FUTURE IS
ROSIE.

Dear Joy

with best wishes

Carolyn May

THE FUTURE IS ROSIE.

a memoir by
CAROLYN MAYLING

Alliance Publishing Press

Alliance Publishing Press

www.alliancepublishingpress.com

Published by Alliance Publishing Press Ltd
This paperback edition published 2023
Copyright © Carolyn Mayling 2023
Carolyn Mayling asserts her moral right to be
identified as the author of this book.

ISBN: 978-1-8382598-3-9

Typeset in Adobe Garamond Pro
Book & Cover Design by **WORKSHOP**65.co.uk

Biography

Carolyn studied at Arts Educational Schools focussing on performing arts. This early training led her to successfully audition for several national theatre and television shows under her maiden name Carolyn Keston.

These theatrical experiences fuelled Carolyn's passion for coaching young performers. She began teaching at Redroofs School for the Performing Arts, which her mother June had founded in 1947. The dedicated and professional tuition offered by Carolyn and her family have helped launch the careers of many Oscar and BAFTA award winning artistes in Film, Television and Theatre.

Carolyn married David Mayling in 1987. Together they had two daughters Ellie in 1988 and Rosie in 1991 both of whom loved the arts and attended Redroofs.

Following the tragic death of their younger daughter Rosie in 2003 aged just eleven, they honoured her wish to help sick children by founding Rosie's Rainbow Fund.

The registered charity offers music therapy for sick children, support for parents with children in hospital and bereavement services for parents who have lost a child. Over the years many thousands of children and families have benefitted from Rosie's legacy.

In 2008, five years after the loss of her daughter, and with the help of IVF, Carolyn and David had a son Dominic. She was fifty-four years of age.

Carolyn was awarded a Point of Light in 2015 by former Prime Minister David Cameron for "outstanding volunteering in the service of others".

In 2017 Carolyn was invited to speak about her charity work at the Classic FM Live concert performed at the Royal Albert Hall.

Now divorced, Carolyn lives in Berkshire with her teenage son Dominic, near to daughter Ellie, and her two grandchildren. She continues to run Redroofs School for the Performing Arts and Rosie's Rainbow Fund.

Her memoir *The Future is Rosie* is her first published work.

For my three children
Ellie, Rosie and Dominic.

Contents

Prologue
August 2004

In the barn a contented sow was lying with her new-born piglets.

I leant against the wall of the stall and closed my eyes for a moment. The straw was damp, and pungent, but it smelt like nature and the quietness was soothing. I listened to the rain beating a staccato tap dance on the corrugated barn roof and then became aware of the soft snuffling near my feet. I blinked and watched as the eight little new-borns rooted for their mother's milk.

I suddenly felt a sharp tug at my heart and a primeval longing for this warmth.

I was jealous! How sad was that to feel jealous of a pig? But watching the sow with her little black and pink spotty miracles, I heard the voice in my head. It was Rosie's voice, clear, piping, and forthright as it always was, saying, "You can do this too."

It seemed patently obvious, and Rosie was always right.

Cornwall
August 1995

We were on holiday at a Cornish seaside hotel with our girls. It was a carefree, messing about with buckets and spades holiday, our little family of four doing all the normal stuff that families do on a summer break.

They paddled in the sea, bounced around in the hotel soft play, bounced around some more on the beds, and then, exhausted after another day on the breezy Cornish beach, splashed in a bubble bath together, singing musical theatre numbers at the tops of their voices.

"Come on, girls, into bed NOW!" I ordered.

"Daddy, tell us the story about Steven the Rat?" Rosie begged.

"Not Steven the Rat again." I laughed.

David's rat story was his pièce de résistance. While I read to the girls at home every bedtime, where they enjoyed everything from Roald Dahl to Frances Hodgson Burnett, he would make up adventures which involved a dastardly rodent who got into increasingly alarming situations.

"Yes, again. Come on, Daddy, tell us the one about when Steven gets stuck down the toilet."

"Once upon a time there was a rat, and he was called Steven the Rat, and he had a friend who was called Steven the Hedgehog!"

Rosie would find these tales hilarious and David's bedtime stories would hype them up until they were high as kites and Rosie would dissolve in hiccoughs from laughing. Then I would spoil their fun, saying it was time to settle down. I would brush the sand off the bed and hang their little damp swimsuits out on the balcony to dry in the cool salty Cornish air.

Looking for something grown-up to do one evening, we spotted a list of events on the hotel notice board.

Wednesday Events.

Psychic Medium Readings by appointment.

For want of anything else to do and just for a laugh, I booked a slot and the hotel baby-sitting service. We checked our sleeping beauties. Ellie, aged seven, was Snow White pretty, her long dark hair neat on the pillow, while Rosie, aged four, was the wrong way up as usual, her untamed brown curls still harbouring grains of sandy beach where she hadn't let me brush it. Both were sound asleep, so we took the lift to the hotel lounge.

The medium beckoned us over to a table in the corner. "Do you mind if I write it down?" I asked.

"Not at all, dear."

She was coming to the end of the psychic reading when she suddenly looked at me. Well, not actually at me but past me somewhere over my left shoulder.

"I see a child. I see two children already on this earth plane, but this is not one of them. This is another child who will be coming to you after a very long gap."

I shrugged. "Well, it must be a grandchild then because there is no way we are planning any more children."

"No, dear," she insisted, "this is not a grandchild. This is your child, and it will be coming to you after a very long time."

"No chance," we said dismissively. Our family was complete. Our lives were already hectic and busy. David was building extensions and my life was always jammed full of running our theatre school with my mum and Sam, my sister. There was no way we would start again with nappies and night feeds.

I scribbled the medium's predictions into a notebook, which I stuffed into the pocket of my suitcase, and gave it no more thought.

After the holiday, when we came home, I tidied the notebook away. It remained stashed under a pile of papers in a box in the back of a cupboard where it was forgotten about.

Setting the Scene
1965

My parents' white country house nestles in a small horseshoe-shaped hamlet just outside Maidenhead. Redroofs was once home to the late theatrical impresario Ivor Novello. With hundreds of years of history, it even has the lilac tree in the garden which inspired Ivor's famous song 'We'll Gather Lilacs in the Spring'. Mum has countless books and albums of old photos of famous theatricals from the 1930s and '40s wandering the gardens and attending Ivor's many elaborate musical garden parties. Stars of stage and screen, such as Laurence Olivier, Margaret Rutherford, Vivien Leigh, and Noël Coward, would frequent Redroofs in those pre-World War Two days. Redroofs has such a wealth of theatre history that when my mother discovered it for sale in 1965, she was immediately hooked even though the house was in a state of disrepair.

Grandpa Max, who had significant experience in the property market, took a trip from Edgware to Maidenhead to offer his expert opinion. Leaving the safe boundaries of his community, he made no secret of the fact he was less than impressed that Mum and Dad wanted to leave a nice Jewish London suburb to consider living in a place in the country where you couldn't even buy a loaf of chollah or gefilte fish balls!

Grandpa Max surveyed the house and large garden at Redroofs, shook his head disdainfully, and, in his self-made businessman's strong Polish accent, remarked, "Ach, June, vot you vont this for? But it voot make a nice block of flats."

Dad had originally wanted to move out of London to live on the banks of the River Thames in order that he could moor his little cabin cruiser.

Redroofs was not near a river, but Mum had already fallen head over heels in love with the house and her mind was made up.

My dad Phillip, my mum June, pregnant with Samantha, myself age ten and two younger brothers Ludovic and Robin upped sticks in 1965 and moved from Cricklewood Northwest London to leafy Berkshire. Mum, who had already spent years establishing a popular theatre school in Cricklewood, turned part of Redroofs into a theatre school. Later she and Dad converted a section of the house into a mini theatre furnished with forty-two discarded red velvet seats from the Theatre Royal Windsor.

The drama and dance class lists expanded quickly, and she was soon filling classes every evening and weekend with aspiring pint-size actors and young performers. The school was so busy that she eventually closed the Cricklewood branch and concentrated on Redroofs Theatre School in Maidenhead.

While we were living in Northwest London, I successfully auditioned for a full-time theatre school Arts Educational based at Hyde Park Corner and attended there from 1962–1964. I loved it there, travelling to school on the number 16 bus from Cricklewood Broadway to Marble Arch. I took ballet lessons in a high-ceilinged studio overlooking the statue of Queen Boadicea and, because I was small for my age, was regularly selected for photographic modelling assignments featuring on the front of knitting patterns. I revelled in those outings from school. In the charge of a chaperone, I would skip out of arithmetic lessons and onto the tube at Green Park to the photographic studios with a small group of excited children.

After moving to Maidenhead, Mum and Dad sent me to boarding school at the sister school in Hertfordshire. I was reluctant to board, but Mum sold it to me with the promise that there would be midnight feasts Enid Blyton style and by describing the adventures she herself experienced when she had been evacuated in 1939 to a boarding school in a castle in North Wales.

So, I started there in January 1965 after we moved to Maidenhead. For some reason Ludovic, Robin, and Samantha went to local schools, but I was sent off at the age of ten with my trunk, a long list of items labelled with Cash's name tapes, and a large writing set for writing letters home. Although I suffered increasing homesickness being sent away from Mum, Dad, and my younger siblings, I did have the good fortune of auditioning and being selected for some exciting professional engagements. At twelve I was cast as Barry Humphries' daughter in *The Late Show* for BBC. This was followed by dancing most of the children's roles in *The Nutcracker* with the English National Ballet. I appeared with the company at the Royal Festival Hall and on tour for three consecutive years.

Leaving school at seventeen, I was immediately cast as Therese Strauss in the TV series *The Strauss Family*.

However, my dance opportunities during my *Nutcracker* years fuelled my passion for training young performers and I began teaching at Mum's school. We invested endless passion, time, and energy into the family business.

When we lived in London, Dad ran a club called The Coronet in St John's Wood. It had been a popular social meeting place for Jewish youngsters. When we moved to Maidenhead, Dad closed the club and turned to antique dealing. While Mum was teaching speech and drama, he opened an antique shop in Windsor. He would go around buying and selling old clocks and bronzes, becoming quite an authority on the subject.

In 1976, at twenty-one, I met a musician called Jim and we decided to get married. It quickly became apparent he did not want children. I tried to convince myself he would change his mind later and in those days when a big wedding was booked, the dress bought, and everything organised, it wasn't the done thing to cancel, so in June 1980 we married.

In 1981 the theatre school had become so popular that the business purchased another building nearby in Maidenhead, where we set up a full-time theatre school which we named Redroofs Theatre School.

My marriage to Jim ended and in 1984 I met a builder called David, a down to earth man who wanted children. Meanwhile in the back of Exchange and Mart, Mum had spotted the leasehold of a disused cinema near Ascot and snapped it up, planning to convert it into a small working theatre. David, being a builder, scored a wheelbarrow full of brownie points by enlisting the help of his brothers, Kenny, Dennis, Colin, and Nigel, who were also handy with a hammer. Together they converted the cinema into the Novello Theatre. We ran a theatre company there, providing employment for performers trained through our school and opportunities for talented Redroofs pupils.

David and I married in 1987. Our daughter Ellie was born in 1988, followed by Rosie in 1991. Sadly, Dad died three years later after a long illness.

The girls loved the Novello, decorated in the style of a Victorian Pollock's toy theatre, and adored the colourful theatrical personalities who performed there. They would watch all the shows from the back of the stalls. It was normal for them to play with the props, tear tickets with 'Aunty' Diana, who ran our box office, or help to sell programmes and hang out backstage with the actors. The theatre was their playroom, and they were never happier than when they were making up shows. As they grew up Ellie loved to dance and was a graceful ballet dancer while Rosie made it very clear at her first ballet lesson that she had her own ideas. At her first dance class, aged just two and three quarters, she marched into the middle of the circle of baby ballerinas and declared loudly, "I am not doing ballet anymore; I am going shopping." However, she revelled in the dressing up, acting, and all the camaraderie and creative side of our showbiz world.

Why Don't You Hop?
1996

Rosie on Film Set

When Rosie was just five, she was cast as Ariadne Wetherby, the daughter of the Unknown Soldier in a wartime TV series. Another of our pupils, Dani, was cast as her twin sister. They looked very much alike although Dani was two years older. Although they were not related, they both had dimpled round faces and chestnut curls. It was the second time they had been cast as twins. Just a few months before, they had played twins in an episode of BBC's *Pie in the Sky*.

We were on a location shoot at a rather beautiful old manor house somewhere near Oxford. There were many real-life amputees cast as extras and playing wounded World War One soldiers. Outside in a large walled garden, thirty men, fully costumed with plenty of fake blood, grimy bandages, and war wounds applied by the make-up department, were lined up in rows on old-fashioned stretchers set along an old red brick wall.

Rosie emerged from the hair and make-up Winnebago dressed in a white Edwardian period style dress with a wide blue sash and a large floppy hat pinned over her long brown curls. I wondered how long she would keep it attached on this unusually windy day, but for now she looked unusually pristine and angelic. She was ready for her scene and waiting for her take. She had hop-scotched along the old path looking for something to do to pass some time, where she encountered a horizontal amputee soldier and was eyeing him curiously. As it turned out he had lost his leg in a motor bike accident. He was lying on his stretcher, in military costume with his stump in full view, eating a Mars Bar and reading a newspaper. Turning her attention from the Mars Bar to the stump and then to him, she chirped, "Why don't you get up off that stretcher and come and play with me?"

He lowered his newspaper to his chest and smiled. "I can't walk; I only have one leg!"

She answered, "Well, why don't you hop?" Rosie, who was forthright and a problem solver even at five years old, just figured that a hopping game with an amputee around the film set was a no-brainer. She was disappointed that she never got to see if he could hop as she was called to set, where the wind lifted her hat off mid-take. The director thought it added charm to the scene, so they left that bit in!

At that time, she was attending a small local prep school, while Ellie, age eight, had already started as a full-time pupil at our theatre school. Rosie, at five, made no secret that she wanted to join too, but I explained she was too young and would have to stay there for three more years.

'Grandma's' School
1998

By the time she was seven, Rosie was complaining regularly and bitterly that normal school was boring and that she was fed up and wanted to go to 'Grandma's' school.

Rosie's academic work had started to slip. Slashes across her work in red ballpoint were upsetting her and so a meeting was arranged with her class teacher, who advised me to make an appointment for her to be tested for dyslexia.

All the way in the car, Rosie grumbled, "I am NOT dyslexic; I'm just bored and fed up. Mummy, I mean it. If I can't go to Grandma's school, I'm going to run away to London and go to stage school there."

Arriving at the Dyslexia Institute, Rosie scowled at me over her shoulder as she was escorted by a middle-aged gentleman into the testing room. Completing the test in record time, she bounded back into the waiting room grinning, followed by the man with a clip board and a pile of graphs and sheets bearing the outcome. "Mrs Mayling," he said, "Rosie's results show that she is absolutely not dyslexic. Also, her IQ test shows she sits in the top 10% of all school-age children in the UK."

"You see?" exclaimed my small dramatic daughter indignantly. "I TOLD you I was not dyslexic; I am just bored. NOW can I leave my school and go to Grandma's school?"

She started at 'Grandma's' school the next term. There were no more red crosses in her books. She ecstatically embraced theatre school and, although she was the youngest in the school, quickly made her presence felt.

Rosie kept her classmates well entertained with her escapades. She would be the one to dare the boys to perform Moonies at the back of the coach on school trips. In the classroom the staff warmed to her natural curiosity and ability to learn. Her drama teachers were impressed by her imagination, sense of comedy, and ability to communicate with children and adults equally.

There were plenty of opportunities to perform with regular shows and an annual professional pantomime.

At the Novello Theatre, she would sneak into the principal artistes' dressing rooms while performing in panto to take them their favourite chocolates, smuggled under her costume from the front of house theatre bar. Rosie was the cheeky one, always in the wings planning jokes on the adult cast, making them corpse onstage during the shows. Even the theatre chaperones were amused, but while she was a bundle of fun, she always took her performances seriously, never missing a cue.

She and my mother enjoyed a close bond. Rosie would often be found sitting beside her grandma during rehearsals. This little assistant director would jot notes and suggest improvements while Mum directed the shows. They would sit together in the stalls in row H, seats 7 and 8. Rosie claimed that H8 was her seat.

At home we added two cats and a Golden Retriever puppy to the household.

Daisy quickly became Rosie's cat and Doodle Ellie's. The girls made impressive costumes for them. Tessie the puppy was named after Tessie the crybaby orphan from *Annie* the musical because Ellie had recently played the role in a professional production. Tessie and Rosie became inseparable and were often wrapped around each other. Her most normal position was crouched down and entwined with Tessie.

Rosie, Ellie and Tessie

Idyllic family days came and went with the passing seasons. As the girls grew, so did our extended family. Soon Ellie and Rosie were part of the gaggle of ten cousins.

Ellie, Rosie, Harriet, Alice, Cordelia, twins Emily and Laura-Jane, Molly-May, Rowan, and Sasha were all bright, smart, and mostly stage struck. Ten female cousins who relished being in each other's company.

On summer Sundays the clans would descend to Mum's house and Redroofs would be filled with the sound of laughing children. On these family days, the speciality dessert was my sister-in-law Fiona's raspberry pavlova. We would all congregate in the kitchen while Fiona would assemble the meringue, cream, and raspberries, and the kids devoured quantities of Rocket ice lollies raided from the freezer. Mum's granddaughters would splash in her pool while we sat and dined al fresco. Then the girls would play hide and seek around her house, dripping water on the carpets.

In winter there were more family days, Christmases, and elaborately made-up shows starring the cousins, with most of them arguing over who would take on the role of director.

They would disappear upstairs to ransack the sprawling costume department. This was housed in one wing of Mum's house. Mum never threw anything away, so it was packed floor to ceiling with costumes from school and company shows dating back to 1947. We always found it amusing that she hoarded boxes full of old faded nylon leotards from the early '60s, tutus with torn net, old tatty shirts with every shape collar imaginable, and hundreds of pantomime and show costumes bearing name tapes of every child who had worn the costume over decades. There was even a four-legged Daisy the Cow on a hanger, stuffed in between Red Riding Hood's red cape and various heavy velvet robes and a room full of wedding dresses which were donated to her when a local wedding shop closed after a flood and so many were watermarked. Mum's wartime *make do and mend* outlook meant that she never disposed of anything and maintained that everything would come in useful at some point.

The cousins would rummage through boxes labelled *chicken knickers*, *tights assorted*, *orphans*, *dance festival singles*, *wigs short* and *wigs long*, *toppers*, and *berets*. Rosie would try to carry piles of costumes and props downstairs. "Help me carry these costumes downstairs; I'm mounded," Rosie would say. She and the kids would surface in an eclectic array of misfitted attire for their latest improvised performance. There were always too many chiefs and not enough Indians, but the shows went on whatever the season with much applause by all the grown-ups dragged from the drawing room or kitchen to watch them.

When it wasn't being used for school holiday course productions and student shows, the cousins would take it over. It was certainly more fun than any board games and their creativity was boundless within these walls of flocked red and gold theatrical wallpaper lit with wonky wall lights.

When I'm Headmistress
1999

One day, age eight, Rosie was in her English lesson when she witnessed one of the teachers make a negative comment to one of her school friends. The child in question was gentle and timid, having been bullied at her previous school. Rosie had voluntarily become this child's minder, promising to fight her corner when necessary.

Rosie, incensed by the injustice, flounced out of the classroom and locked herself in the girls' toilet, staging a one-person sit-in protest.

An hour later she was still refusing to reappear. By lunchtime the whole school had heard about the rumpus, and various members of staff, including the head teacher, were deployed and stationed in a rota outside the door. They had in turn tried talking to her through the locked door. Despite firm tellings-off, coaxing, and attempting every tactic they could think of, Rosie was having none of it.

"When I am headmistress and running this school, things are going to be very different! I am not coming out till she apologises for being unkind to my friend."

Eventually a furious but somewhat exhausted small girl emerged, probably because it was an hour past lunchtime. Strands of long hair were now sprouting out of her ballet bun which had been immaculate that morning, and her face was blotchy from three hours of crossness and a few frustrated tears. She was made to write a formal apology to all the staff.

This was Rosie. She lived her life at speed, always rushing with her foot on the accelerator. Like Anne of Green Gables and Pippi Longstocking all rolled into one, her colourful imagination and sense of justice sometimes landed her in sticky situations. However, she was innately good and kind, always putting others before herself.

Forever and a Day
September 2002

Lucy, Rosie and Laura rehearsing

Our home was always buzzing with kids, sleepovers, music, show songs, and a lot of laughter. Our girls had two special school friends, Lucy and Laura, who were like extended family, and we spent many holidays together. No matter where the children were, whether in Lanzarote, France, Cornwall, or in each other's homes, they would be engrossed in writing shows together. Over time these became more and more elaborate and witty with impressive librettos and scores. Laura would sing and write the librettos, Lucy and Ellie would compose the music, and Rosie would create hilarious lyrics.

Their mum Dee and I had become firm friends over the years and encouraged their creativity, becoming part of their resident 'rent a crowd' audience and offering helpful director's notes, which of course were usually dismissed as they knew how to do it better.

The young impresarios formed a production company. R.E.L.L. Productions stood for Rosie, Ellie, Lucy, and Laura, and they began writing a new musical, *Forever and A Day*, a full-length musical fairy tale. Together with a cast of all-singing, all-dancing kids from the school, they took the show to our Novello Theatre in Ascot where they staged the whole production. Machiel, an outstanding musical and recording artist who taught singing at Redroofs, allowed them to spend time at his studio, where he helped Rosie create a stunning backing track for her song 'Enchanted'.

The children worked hard on the piece and decided between them that proceeds from the performance would go towards raising money for a new wheelchair for Ella, the daughter of Helene, a very dear friend of mine.

Helene and I had been friends for so many years. She had enrolled in our school as a student aged just sixteen and ultimately, after a stint performing professionally, had married Mike, whom she met when he attended one of her Redroofs performances. They had two sons followed by a longed-for daughter. Ella was born seemingly normal, but she was not achieving developmental milestones. She was regressing and Helene and Mike became increasingly worried. Eventually, aged ten months, she was diagnosed with Rett syndrome, a life-limiting neurological genetic disorder. She was as pretty as a porcelain doll with huge blue eyes and a sweet face framed by dark hair. The family did everything they could for their daughter who, despite her disability, clearly loved music and colour. Ella and her whole family attended the performance, and a significant sum of money was raised for her.

At the curtain call, following the applause, Rosie took to the stage with the aplomb and confidence of an assured adult and gave an impromptu speech thanking the cast and the audience for raising funds for Ella's new wheelchair.

Growing Concerns
December 2002

David and I went out for the evening, leaving Ellie and Rosie with their aunty Sam for a sleepover. I had despatched them to her house with overnight bags. They had been eagerly anticipating the stay with their little cousins. Dumping their bags with a "Bye, Mummy, love you, see you tomorrow," they had skipped off happily to play. Sam's characterful brick and flint house overlooking an expanse of Buckinghamshire common was set up for kids, with a cellar converted to a soft play of squashy blocks to jump off into a massive plastic pond filled with coloured balls.

"See you, Caro. I've got popcorn and videos for later. Have fun."

We had driven to a hotel some miles away for an early Christmas party with David's family. We were in the middle of roast turkey with all the trimmings when Sam phoned.

"Nothing to worry about, but Rosie has been sick. She says her tummy hurts, so I have given her some Pepto-Bismol and put her to bed."

Moving away from the noisy gathering to a quieter spot in the hotel lobby, I said, "I'm not unduly worried. It sounds as though she's picked up a winter tummy bug. Kids get them." Sam said she could cope and to come in the morning to collect the girls as planned.

When we arrived to collect the children, Rosie still felt unwell and had a tummy ache.

Driving home to Maidenhead, our normally chatty, exuberant little girl was pale and very quiet. By evening, she was in considerable pain.

We had called the GP, but since her condition was worsening, I took her to A&E at Wexham Park Hospital, leaving David to look after Ellie.

They ran blood tests, which revealed that her markers were raised, indicating a possible infection. A few hours later and unable to diagnose the pain, Rosie was admitted to the paediatric ward 24. David stuffed some overnight things and toothbrushes into a bag and dropped them off.

The nurse said, "This is your bed, Rosie. Mum, you can unfold this bed and sleep next to Rosie." Rosie drifted into an unsettled sleep while I tossed and turned on the creaky camp bed, trying to block out the noise and bustle of the ward, the constant snapping of the metal pedal bins and our new roommates.

There was a boy in the next cubicle. Although there was a curtain between him and us, his mother wandered about opening crisp packets, chewing noisily, and sighing a lot. When she did finally sleep, her snoring kept me awake.

Next morning the consultant on the ward round seemed unconcerned. He was surrounded by a small group of white-coated medical students who had prodded Rosie's tummy. They laughed at the consultant when he suggested, "Well, these kids eat so much pizza at sleepovers that it is probably a case of too much food."

My immediate reaction was one of annoyance, but I accepted that these were professionals and knew best. They discharged her with bottles of laxative and said there appeared to be nothing to be too concerned about.

Rosie was back at school next day. She and Ellie were also starting panto rehearsals for our Christmas show at the Novello Theatre.

Ellie was happily playing dancing roles, while Rosie was looking forward to her little character role of Mini Mean, the sidekick to the baddie in *Puss in Boots*.

She loved character parts. Rosie didn't like the rigidity and constraints of ballet technique nor pale colours or pretty tutus, always opting to audition for the fun cameo roles. She had a penchant for stripes and her wardrobe was full of stripy tights and rainbow-coloured accessories.

Rehearsals were underway. We were relieved that Rosie's tummy pain had subsided.

The girls were loving the build-up to the show and Rosie was also planning her sleepover party for her eleventh birthday on December 17th.

David, the only non-theatrical of the family, endured panto songs day and night. Coming from a family of down to earth builders, he found performers rather embarrassing but would tolerate the kids and their outgoing theatre school friends re-enacting panto scenes round our house.

A few days later Rosie woke up coughing. It was a dry, strange-sounding cough. Her throat was very sore, and she seemed breathless. "I think you should stay home, Rosie. That is a nasty cough, darling. You don't want to be ill for your birthday."

"No way. I have a show to do. I will take some Calpol," said Rosie.

Rosie's cough persisted and her throat was increasingly sore. There were several visits to our GP. She was given an asthma inhaler and antibiotics. By the second week of rehearsals, Rosie was becoming weak and unable to breathe properly. She was determined to continue with her rehearsals for the show, which was due to open soon. But she would stand in the wings gasping, hardly able to deliver her lines or get through a scene.

We insisted that she went home to rest. Much to Rosie's distress, the role of Mini Mean was taken over by her friend.

We organised a referral to a new consultant at Wexham Park Hospital. Again, this consultant was reassuring and diagnosed pneumonia. Rosie was sent home again with yet more antibiotics and an inhaler, and once more we were told not to worry.

The weeks passed and Rosie's cough persisted. She was desperate to get better, and still struggling into school when she could. She went to rehearsals, and we prayed that she would recover from this horrible infection.

Panto opened and Rosie insisted on performing. We had misgivings, but she was desperate to be a part of the show. She managed a couple of performances, but it was clear she simply could not cope. She was gutted. By now our concerns were increasing and our trips to the doctors and hospital became more frequent, but the GP and Rosie's consultant still believed that the medication would work.

Rosie's Birthday
December 17th, 2002

Rosie's eleventh birthday dawned on December 17th, and we had promised she could have a banquet at her favourite local Chinese restaurant with her panto friends, followed by a sleepover. She kept saying she would be fine for the party. We had concerns and suggested to Rosie that we postpone the party until she was better, but she insisted it went ahead because she had already missed out on the fun of most of the rehearsals.

On her birthday she woke up coughing and looking exhausted. She was determined to go, so she spent ages getting ready and even applied some blusher to give her pale cheeks some colour. In her new pink top, stripy pink and purple tights, and denim skirt, she asked me to plait her hair with her new Claire's Accessories hair bobbles and added her pink crocheted hat and favourite gold Doc Marten boots.

She coughed all the way to the restaurant, then greeted her friends, sat at the head of the table, and ordered her favourite crispy duck, acting the perfect host as she always did. Following a rendition of 'Happy Birthday' by the Chinese waiters and the kids, we drove several of the children home for the sleepover.

Eleven-year-olds don't sleep at sleepovers, and some of the kids announced they would be staying awake all night. Rosie put up a brave front, but she was struggling. Pillows were being chucked around the living room, sleeping bags were all over the place, and too many sweets made the kids hyper, but they were having the best time. Rosie wanted to be in the thick of it, but we could see she was quieter than usual.

On the face of it, this was a happy occasion, but I had a terribly uneasy feeling as we listened to Rosie's dry barking cough all night.

By the time Christmas Eve came, Rosie was very weak. There was yet another trip to our GP, who was friendly but dismissive, telling us to "Go home and have a lovely Christmas."

That evening I was wrapping some last-minute gifts. Dee had

popped over with Laura and Lucy for a Christmas Eve drink, so Ellie was happily messing about with them.

"Where's Rosie?" asked Dee. I noticed Rosie, who would normally have been right in the middle of the preparations, had taken herself up to her room and was lying on the bed under her duvet. I went up to check on her. Her heart seemed to be beating very fast, her hands were cold, and her face was pale and clammy. She was agitated and scared.

"Mummy, I am going to die of this!"

My stomach turned over. I was shocked and cross and made no secret of telling her firmly to stop exaggerating.

"Don't be so ridiculous, Rosie. Of course you are not. Stop being a drama queen."

"Mummy, I am. I AM going to die of this!"

Rosie struggled through Christmas Day, putting on her usual brave face and trying so hard to enjoy the day. She had lost weight, had no energy, looked very pale, and the dark rings under her eyes gave her a gaunt look. We even had to help her unwrap her gifts. Even though the medics were not concerned, David and I had a deep sense of unease.

Panto was underway and *Puss in Boots* was playing to good houses. Rosie stayed home, unable to perform or even go and watch the show from the audience.

By New Year we were beyond worried. Dee had been discussing Rosie's symptoms with her stepson, who was a GP. She called me. "He wants to know why on earth the consultant has not done a CT scan. Why have they not tested her?"

Luckily, we had private insurance through our business and so this time I took her back to see the consultant privately.

We had a trip to Barbados planned. David's brother Colin and his Fiancée Niki had arranged their wedding there in March and had asked Ellie and Rosie to be bridesmaids. We had bought them pretty sundresses and they were both excited about the upcoming wedding. I was very worried for Rosie about the impending flight and had becoming jittery about the thought of even sitting on the plane. We wondered how she could endure a long-haul flight when she couldn't even walk from the car park to the consulting room without stopping to gasp for breath.

"The sun will do Rosie good." The consultant smiled.

I asked why Rosie hadn't had a CT scan.

She replied, "You can't just order scans willy nilly."

That was the final straw. I heard myself losing my temper. "As Rosie's mum, I know she is not right, and I want a scan done and I want it done NOW!"

Blue-Lighted
February 2003

Within an hour Rosie was undergoing a CT scan. I insisted on accompanying her into the scan room. They warned me I should not really be present due to risk of radiation, but I was not going to leave her alone. After the scan we were sent back to the waiting area.

Twenty minutes after the results arrived, I was called into the consulting room.

The consultant was trying to maintain her composure, but her smile had disappeared, and she appeared flustered and shaken.

"The CT scan shows pulmonary embolisms, which are clots on the main arteries going into Rosie's lungs. We need to blue-light her to Oxford, immediately. We have arranged for her to be admitted to the paediatric intensive care unit at John Radcliffe Hospital in Oxford."

My stomach turned over.

Rosie's eyes were wide. "In an ambulance?"

She was quite excited by the prospect of going by ambulance.

I made two swift calls, one to David and one to my mother.

Whilst Rosie and I were blue-lighted up the M40, David followed in the car. Rosie joked a little with the paramedic, who was blowing up rubber gloves to make her smile, but my heart was thumping, and I was in shock that the situation had suddenly spiralled from "You can't just order scans willy nilly" to an ambulance racing up the M40 with sirens blaring and Rosie wearing an oxygen mask. We had no idea what lay ahead, but it was clear we were entering totally new territory.

Arriving at John Radcliffe Hospital, we were taken directly to the paediatric intensive care unit. A long corridor led to the PICU. It was very quiet although there were a few children there. Machines were bleeping and there was a nurse assigned to each patient. Rosie was on a stretcher and then transferred to a bed where a nurse introduced herself to us as Shirley.

Shirley was a lively young woman. She joked with Rosie, who by now was sitting up in bed looking more relaxed although she still wore an oxygen mask. Shirley was genuinely interested in Rosie's theatrical pursuits. She was a no-nonsense person with a ready humour, and I was thankful for that, and trusted that Rosie was now in good hands and seemed to have connected with her.

"You need to have some magic cream, Rosie, then we will put a cannula into your hand." They inserted a cannula and put Rosie on IV antibiotics.

She remained in PICU for a few days while a string of doctors tried to work out what was going on. After a few days in PICU, they were none the wiser and Rosie was transferred upstairs onto the children's ward 4B.

The ward back then was shared by young respiratory patients and a lot of oncology patients. We were both stunned to see so many children with no hair who were clearly very sick. Rosie was in a bed opposite a pretty young girl of about her age. She had just been diagnosed with a brain tumour. It was horrifying to see this child and her terrified parents. On the day she arrived, she had long dark hair and a sweet smile. Over the next few days, Rosie witnessed the girl's hair falling out in handfuls until a few days later she was totally bald and looking very ill. There were babies on the ward with serious heart conditions, children with cystic fibrosis, and a lot of other children of all ages in various stages of chemotherapy. Rosie and I considered she was one of the lucky ones and we were thankful that she had so much hair.

Every child on the ward had very stressed parents. This was a hospital where seriously ill patients had been transferred from their local hospitals. These were all very poorly children and the level of worry and fear of all the parents was off the charts. These parents were so involved with their children that not many spoke to or even noticed each other.

We would, however, exchange some brief conversations in the parents' kitchen. It was a poky little room with a small fridge, jars of tea bags, some coffee and sugar, plastic plates, and never enough spoons.

This was the sort of place where you wouldn't want to sit around for long as none of us wanted to be away from our children for more than a couple of minutes.

Each morning Rosie was assessed by different consultants and doctors who poked prodded and asked the same million questions. There were so many blood tests, IV antibiotics, and other tests, some of which were very scary and uncomfortable for her. She developed a fear of cannulas as the intrusive needles were so frequent that her veins were collapsing, so with each new cannula, the procedure became more painful. Rosie saw a cardiologist, a haematologist, and a whole team of doctors attempting to diagnose her condition. But with each test, the results seemed to leave them more confused.

Rosie was placed under the care of Dr Anne Thomson, a paediatric respiratory consultant. Anne was a mature grey-haired Scottish lady with a quiet, unassuming manner and a way of speaking to children on their level, never talking down to them and with a firm belief in honesty at all times. I liked her calm, pragmatic manner. I found out later that Ellie and Rosie had nicknamed her Mrs Doubtfire.

Days and weeks passed and still we waited for a diagnosis. All the days seemed to merge into a strange routine with time measured by medications, new needles, and nurses clocking on and off. Rosie was bored and frustrated. There were more scans, angiograms, and many tears from our increasingly agitated little girl as they fought daily with her fear of cannulas.

Sometimes I would take a quick drive home to do some washing and have a shower in my own bathroom. David would swap places and try to entertain Rosie for a few hours. On one occasion he took in a balloon and newspaper, and they made a papier mâché piggy bank. Rosie painted it bright green and added pink squiggles. It was good for Rosie and her dad to spend time together. Ellie would also visit. It was an ordeal for her. On one hand she was trying to cope with all the usual teenage stuff, but she also wanted time with her little sister and tried to maintain a happy face when she was desperately anxious and powerless to change the worsening situation. Mum visited with flasks of homemade chicken soup which Rosie couldn't face eating. Most of the time and almost every night, David would take Ellie home and look after her whilst I stayed with Rosie on a camp bed by her side.

Fear
March 2003

Four weeks later we were summoned to a meeting in room 22. David and Mum joined me, leaving Rosie in the ward with one of the nurses. This room was known among the other parents on the ward as the *bad news room*. There was nothing in this bare room but tired cream-coloured walls, a hospital pedal bin, a hand basin, and blue plastic NHS chairs.

I was surprised to find Dr Huma, Rosie's old consultant, there too. Seeing how anxious we were, she said, "It will be okay. Everything will be fine." I don't know why she said that knowing what she did, but for a moment my hopes soared. Maybe it would not be so bad.

Dr Anne Thomson, cardiologist Dr Nick Archer, the cardiac respiratory sister, Dr Huma, David, my mother, and I sat in a circle and waited. Dr Thomson looked stressed. "We have a worrying situation. I'm sure I don't need to tell you how serious Rosie's condition is. The embolisms must be removed."

Previously that morning at the ward round, I had asked Dr Archer, "I know this is a silly question, but are these just blood clots or could they be something more sinister?"

Now he cleared his throat. "What you said this morning was not a silly question at all." We forced ourselves to listen as Dr Archer explained that what they had supposed were blood clots on Rosie's pulmonary arteries were maybe malignant tumours. He explained, "We will have to go in and take out whatever they are, do a heart and lung biopsy, and then take appropriate action. We will operate on Wednesday in five days' time."

It was at that moment I realised the full magnitude of what he was saying. I felt sick and couldn't breathe. I wanted to wake up from this nightmare, but it was real. It was the first time I was told of the possibility that Rosie had malignant tumours. We were paralysed with fear. The bottom was falling out of our world. How would we prepare

Rosie for this ordeal? How would we even get through the next few days? I had never been so frightened. Anne Thomson volunteered to tell Rosie.

They left the room and I collapsed. It was as though I was watching myself from outside my body, looking down at a woman who reminded me of me, bent double, making a hideous moaning noise. I was pulled up sharply by Mum telling me to hold myself together and be strong for Rosie. She mustn't see our panic. I recall shuffling down the hospital corridor like an old woman towards Rosie's bed.

Rosie immediately knew something was up. "What's going on? Where have you been? You've been gone ages!" Anne Thomson explained gently that she would have to have an operation. "I don't want an operation. Mummy, Daddy, I don't want an operation." She was frightened and I did a useless job of consoling her.

The next five days were hell. David walked me to the hospital surgery, where they prescribed diazepam. At night when Rosie was asleep, and I was lying staring at her from my camp bed in a state of panic and fear, I would take a diazepam to knock me out. David and Mum were trying to be positive. Things would be alright. The hospital would sort Rosie out. Mum had always been my rock and I tried to believe her.

It was during these few days that I had the premonition. An image kept appearing in my mind. It was like a vision as I knew I was awake. I saw Rosie's funeral. A crematorium, the flowers on a coffin, the light wooden colour of a box, and clearest of all I heard the song 'Enchanted', Rosie's song that she had written for the musical *Forever and A Day*, which now seemed as though it had been in some other distant life. I tried so hard to block the images, but they lodged themselves in my head in full technicolour.

Each evening when Mum, David, and Ellie left the hospital, I would pace up and down the corridors and, when Rosie drifted to sleep, would creep out of the ward, going downstairs to a paved area outside. It was cold and grey, smelling of cigarettes, and felt like the area inside a prison wall where inmates took their exercise. This was where stressed, pale parents dialled home on their mobiles. There were lots of us there. Some were pregnant with problems and waiting for their babies to arrive, but most like me were parents of long-term patients. I would make my evening phone calls to the family and close friends. They were desperate for good news and to hear that Rosie was feeling better, but I was unable to sound optimistic. Exhausted from fear and anxiety and weak from loss of appetite, the pounds were dropping off me.

After the evening calls, I would go back to the ward, try and grab a quick shower in the dingy shared bathroom, and then attempt to sleep on the camp bed next to Rosie. If Rosie was on the general bay and not in a side room, it was impossible to sleep. There was constant activity throughout the night. Nurses moving around the ward, doing observations, pushing drip stands around, talking to other staff, and working hard in the dim light. It was never dark and there were always children crying.

On one particular night I locked myself in the parents' toilet, trying to stop shaking and remain calm for Rosie. Leonie the cardiac sister knocked on the door and asked if I would like to talk to her. She knew what a state I was in. "You need to look after the kids, not me. I'm okay. I'm okay, honestly." I was sobbing.

"Carolyn, you can talk to me. I can see you are not okay."

I described the premonition to her. She looked very shocked and told me not to think like that. Leonie had children to look after, and I could not take up any more of her time.

But there was no support or counselling for parents like me who so badly needed comforting and a trained ear. I felt very alone at this time.

Rosie was also very worried. She had several visits from the doctors, the anaesthetist, and nurses, who spent time explaining and reassuring her. I kept praying all the time, "Please don't let it be a tumour." Everything else paled into insignificance. If it wasn't a tumour, then everything would be alright.

In the nights leading up to the operation, I would try to read to

Rosie. I could hardly breathe and found it a struggle to get the words out. After she was asleep, I would lean against the window and try to breathe some fresh air through the window crack. They would never open far enough, and it was always stuffy. I would look out at the normal world going on beyond the perimeters of the hospital. There were ordinary families outside doing ordinary things. I could see the lights in their windows and imagined how they would be bathing their kids, cooking an evening meal, watching TV. That world seemed so distant and all those things I used to get stressed over just seemed insignificant now. If only Rosie would get better, I would never complain about anything ever again. I spent a lot of time praying, wishing, and even bargaining with God.

"Dear God, if you make Rosie better, I will do anything, literally anything, but please just get us through this and back to the normal life which I never fully appreciated till now."

I can't remember much else except visits from David, Ellie, Mum, Sam, and close friends. Ellie was clearly worried. She was much quieter than usual, and I was unable to connect with her. When David took her and Mum home after each visit, it was really difficult and compounded the intense and frightening isolation I felt.

Eventually Wednesday came. Rosie was restless and agitated and wouldn't take the pre-med.

"I'm not drinking that; it's disgusting and it's green."

"Please, Rosie, just drink it, please?"

"No."

It was unfortunate as it contained a sedative which might have helped to calm her. Eventually when she did decide to have it, it was too late and had no effect.

The porter arrived to collect Rosie and we accompanied her down to theatre. We both tried to sound upbeat so Rosie would not sense our fear. She was astute and perceptive at the best of times and this morning she sensed our anxiety and was clearly terrified.

The operation went ahead, and David and I were advised to drive home for a couple of hours to try to pass the time. Just doing something was better than doing nothing, but it was a very long few hours. Having reached home, we were unsettled and agitated, roaming around the house watching the clock, making cups of tea we couldn't swallow, and attempting to eat a sandwich which made us gag.

When we returned, Dr Phil Roberts met us outside the lift. He was smiling. He reported that Rosie was now out of theatre, and it looked like a blood clot. They were 99.9% sure it was clot. The haematologist confirmed the news. Rosie was in recovery. The operation had gone well. We were ecstatic. Just a clot and the clot had been removed. It was as though a huge weight had lifted. We went to the local pub just beyond the entrance to the hospital and ordered steak and chips. I felt hungry for the first time in weeks.

Rosie was in PICU for twenty-four hours, being cared for by Shirley, and then they moved her back up to the children's ward. She was very sore with a long scar which, although bandaged, stretched from her neck to lower diaphragm.

"Mummy, you lied to me. You said it wouldn't hurt." Rosie was distraught and in so much pain whilst I was mortified that she thought we had lied to her. We all reassured her that her scar would fade and would be under her bra by the time she was old enough to wear one.

The next day Dr Adwani came and did an echocardiogram. He was bright and breezy and joked with Rosie as he spread the gel on her chest. Jelly belly, he called it.

He was moving the prong around her chest and looking at the image on the screen which he had wheeled to the side of her bed.

Suddenly he went very quiet. "What do you see?" I asked.

"I will finish the echo and then talk," he said without looking at me. After a few minutes, which seemed like an eternity, he pointed to some shadows on the screen. "That is clot," he said. He was shaking his head and frowning. "The clots. They have come back."

Twenty-four hours after the major and difficult operation which should have sorted out the problem, the clots had returned. Now all the team were puzzled and worried. They had never seen a condition like this in a child. They began to run more tests. There seemed to be a hotline between her consultants and various other hospitals. There was talk of transferring her to Papworth in Cambridge or Great Ormond Street. There were calls between Rosie's doctors and eminent medics all over the world. Rosie was subjected to the most unpleasant investigations. Dyes were injected into her; blood was taken so often that she was looking like a little pincushion. MRI scans, CT scans, eye tests.

And then after what seemed an eternity, there was a diagnosis. Rosie had vasculitis, a rare autoimmune disease. The problem was not with the blood but with the blood vessels. Anne Thomson told us the condition was treatable but first they must narrow the field down to try to discover which form of vasculitis she was suffering from. This meant that Rosie had to spend more time in hospital.

Many friends came to visit. Among them Gaenor, whose own daughter had spent the first year of her life in intensive care. She knew how important it was to offer practical help, bringing in lovely hand cream to soften my sore hands from constant washing to keep hospital bugs at bay.

Another friend, Candice, brought homemade shepherd's pies to heat up in the parents' kitchen. And Helene was always there listening and looking after me.

After many days of waiting and trying to fill the interminable hours, we were told that they were still undecided, but that treatment would start that very afternoon.

The treatment for vasculitis was steroids and anti-coagulants. I remember expressing concern to Anne Thomson about Rosie becoming moonfaced. She was quick to tell me that the most important thing was that Rosie got well.

The next month dragged by. Rosie had played every video and game in the hospital playroom. She was bored and bad-tempered. I noticed the steroids were changing the shape of her face. On the upside they were increasing her appetite and she ordered chicken nuggets and fries, which David would bring in from the McDonald's on the corner near the exit from the M40. The days were long and there was nothing to do. She was desperate to see her school friends and we were both very pleased when we heard that her friends Sophie and Joe were coming to visit.

The Simpsons
April 2003

Rosie was at the end of a very tiring day and had undergone some unpleasant tests. The one saving grace was that two of her school friends were due to arrive for a visit at around 6.45pm.

She had been waiting all day for Dr Archer, who was conducting her daily scans. He was very late, eventually sending for her to go down for a scan at 6pm. It was *The Simpsons* time, which she eagerly looked forward to every day, so Rosie was furious and refused to go. Eventually she was cajoled into it, and I took her in a wheelchair to locate Dr Archer. When we arrived downstairs Dr Archer was greeted by a very indignant, cross Rosie saying, "I HAVE to watch *The Simpsons*, Dr Archer. It's my absolute favourite and you were supposed to be here earlier."

He agreed that he was indeed a bit late and instructed the nurses to find a room with a TV and a scanner so she could watch *The Simpsons* downstairs in the scan room. So, Dr Archer and various nurses were running around the hospital looking for a TV which worked. He was trying to be patient and to keep his sense of humour after a very long day with other patients, but Rosie was getting more and more frustrated as time crept on. Eventually, a room was found, but the TV was not working. Rosie missed *The Simpsons* and was very put out. A nurse tried to be helpful by offering *Mr Blobby* instead. Dr Archer apologised to her profusely, but Rosie was fed up and upset.

Joe and Sophie were stationed expectantly by her bed when she finally arrived back on the ward. Rosie was overjoyed to see them. The contrast between her and her healthy, active friends was huge. She looked a shadow of her old self. They were eager to use the short time they had with her and asked me if they could take her for a tour round the hospital. I had reservations but said they could.

It was the happiest visit for Rosie. They ran to the lifts with her in a wheelchair and spent a manic hour racing round the hospital, and this lifted her spirits. I could see a little of the old cheeky child return as she reconnected with her buddies for a short time. To hear her laugh meant everything and helped to pass another interminable evening.

The next day word had spread on the hospital staff grapevine that this little girl had managed to get everyone running rings trying to sort things out. As Rosie's nurse flushed her cannula and did her obs, she exclaimed in a loud whisper, "Oh my gosh, you are the talk of the hospital this morning, Rosie. Dr Archer is a bit like God in this hospital. Did you know he writes and publishes books? He is a very important and really rather famous man."

Rosie was completely unimpressed and shrugged her shoulders. "Well, I wanted to watch *The Simpsons* and I missed it!"

Rosie would regularly ask me when she could go home and back to school. There was nothing to do during those endless days. The children on ward 4B were seriously ill, many undergoing aggressive cancer treatments, so it was not really the most conducive environment in which to foster friendships between the children. There was a schoolteacher who would do some academic teaching with the children who were well enough. This was spasmodic as a lot of the time the children were simply not up to it.

One day Rosie was in the hospital playroom. We were with Christine, who was the lead play specialist, passing another dull and uninspiring morning. Christine was a dedicated and experienced member of the staff and over the time we had been in hospital, we had become friendly. Her niece was a musical theatre performer, so we had a lot of common ground to talk about. It was refreshing and grounding to be able to have a conversation about theatre. Rosie looked up from her colouring and suddenly announced, "I've been thinking… When I am better, I am going to put on shows to raise money for the children in the hospital."

"What a great idea," said Christine.

Easter with the Cousins
April 2003

It was Easter and Rosie was allowed out for a day release. Our family had arranged to drive from the hospital to my brother Robin's house. Rosie's uncle Robin and aunty Helen had gone to a lot of trouble to organise a wonderful family day with all of Rosie's nine cousins, who had made a *Welcome Rosie* banner which they held up as we drove into their drive from the hospital. Rosie was so weak we had borrowed a wheelchair and an oxygen canister from the hospital.

She was so brave that day. She couldn't keep up with the others on the Easter egg hunt around their garden. Ellie, pushing that awful chair and cumbersome oxygen cylinder, was the only one who completely understood how hard it was for Rosie, who was lagging behind as the excited cousins were finding their Easter eggs first.

The twins Emily and Laura-Jane had a zip wire, and all the children were whizzing from end to end, laughing and excited. But Rosie never complained; she was just happy to be with her sister and cousins again. They all looked healthy and robust, which made me realise how frail and pale she was.

It was a huge effort for her to get through that day. It tore me apart to witness my little girl out in the sunshine for the first time in months, refusing to let anyone know how much she was struggling. Robin and Helen were shocked at how ill she looked. We did our best to enjoy the elaborate lunch which Helen had gone to such trouble to prepare. Rosie sat at the table in her wheelchair. I was gutted for her.

The exertion made her breathless, and she was exhausted when we arrived back on the ward that evening. Her saturation levels had dropped quite low, and they had to increase the oxygen, so she was back to wearing the mask. It seemed that any time she went out of the hospital even for a few hours, the effort would set her back. The stark contrast between her and the lively, thriving cousins as they ran and danced around the garden was hard to bear.

One week later on April 28th, 2003, she was finally discharged. We had been praying for this day for so long and were so excited to pack the bags and clear out the little hospital cupboard by her bed for the last time. Rosie even said she would miss the nurses and was quite emotional and sentimental as we said thank you and goodbye to the staff. She said a personal farewell to her favourite nurses and a gentle goodbye to the few parents we had forged a bit of a bond with.

Although she was still weak, the doctors hoped that eventually she would regain strength and be well enough to return to school.

It felt surreal to have her home after so many months removed from the real world, and she was overjoyed to be back with Ellie and some semblance of normality. It was a joyful homecoming, but despite being so happy to be home, Rosie had no strength.

The Swing
May 2003

"I really want to go to Charlotte's for Bank Holiday Monday, Mummy. Please, I really want to go, and I will be fine."

I felt terribly nervous and had an overwhelming need to wrap her up in cotton wool.

It was Sunday, May 5th, 2003, and Rosie had been home for just six days. "I'm not sure, but maybe we can go just for a little while, Rosie. I can hang around at her house and wait for you. I could stay and have a coffee with Charlotte's mum and then I can bring you home."

"It's just so unfair. Why can't I go on my own? I will be fine," she grumbled.

Rosie was so fed up. She was sick of being sick, and tired of having her freedom curtailed for months on end. She was desperate to spend normal time with her friends without having someone monitoring every move. She hadn't visited Charlotte for many months. The last time was before she became ill, and they had enjoyed such a happy day and she had come back covered in chocolate with a large bag of homemade treats from hours of fudge making in Charlotte's kitchen.

She looked bitterly disappointed. I felt guilty constraining my daughter after she had been so trapped, locked away, and unable to control anything. She just wanted to be like any other eleven-year-old. I felt deeply uneasy but also accepted I was totally exhausted and perhaps not able to judge effectively.

"I'm going outside," she said with a sigh.

She went into the garden. I was pleased that she wanted to be outdoors in the sunshine.

Everything was blossoming into flower. Our garden was untidy from the long months of neglect while we were at the hospital, but there were daffodils, and the grass was lush. The Wendy house was looking a bit worse for wear, but I made a mental note to smarten it up now that she was home, and we could plant window boxes at the front of the little windows. We would visit the garden centre and buy some trailing blue lobelia, which would look lovely, and we could add some geraniums and marigolds. It was surely just a matter of time for her to regain strength, breathe fresh warm spring air into her damaged lungs, and bring colour back into her pale cheeks. This was a step towards normality.

"I'm going on my swing, Mum," she called.

"Okay, but please just be careful!"

"I will!"

She made her way to her swing at the end of the garden. I could see that she was quite slow and kept stopping to take a breath. In the last six months, the only time it had moved was when the wind caught it empty, and now it was ready and waiting, so Rosie tentatively sat on the red seat.

Then she started to swing. I watched through the kitchen window. Her leggings were baggy where she had lost weight and her legs looked as skinny and weak as Bambi as she pushed them back and forth and back and forth and swung higher and higher.

I ran after her into the garden.

"Rosie, slow down, please. You are going too high."

I was trying to grab the back of the swing to slow it down, but just for a moment she was flying. She was airborne and shouted to me in no mean terms,

"DON'T LIMIT MY LIFE. I DON'T WANT TO BE LIMITED IN ANY WAY."

The thought of a life full of limits was more than she could bear. So, on the understanding that I would go along, we made a tentative arrangement for the next day. Charlotte's mum was happy for me to go too, and Rosie reluctantly had to accept it was the way it had to be – at least until she grew stronger.

"Can I watch *I'm a Celebrity*, Mum?"

"Of course you can, but bed straight after," I said.

Later that evening, she was snuggled on the sofa with David. It was like old times –almost.

From the kitchen I could hear Rosie and David laughing together as they watched ITV's *I'm a Celebrity Get Me Out of Here.* I told myself to be thankful she was home and tried to relax as I loaded the dishwasher and washing machine, leaving them to make up for some of the daddy and daughter time which they had missed so much.

Ellie had gone off to a sleepover with her friend. She was overjoyed to have her sister home but needed her own life back too. Her fourteenth year had been anything but normal. The guilt I felt for all the time I had not given to her over the last months was weighing heavily on my conscience. She needed to start to relax, and to be with her friends, so she had left happily to spend the night.

Rosie's high-pitched giggle warmed my heart. It was just a matter of time until things would be normal, until I could stop worrying, until I could feel at peace. With every day that passed, Rosie would get stronger, and we could soon return to our carefree lives, to the old normal. We never appreciated how simple life used to be back then.

That night I slept fitfully, tiptoeing into Rosie's room a few times during the night to check on her breathing. Rosie was sleeping. David was already asleep, so I tried too.

This Must Be What Hell Is
May 6th Bank Holiday, 2003

At 6.30 next morning I sleepily turned over to see Rosie standing by the door of our bedroom.

She was leaning against the door frame. Her purple satin pyjamas seemed way too big now. "Mummy," she said, "don't get up. I've had enough of bed, so I'm just going downstairs to play on the computer."

"Okay, darling, that's fine. Put your dressing gown on."

"You don't need to come down. I'll get some Shreddies," she said.

I heard her padding downstairs and smiled to myself and although I wished she had slept a little longer, I closed my eyes, drifting into a semi-sleep, enjoying the calm. David was still asleep and did not stir. The sound of coughing shook me awake with a jolt. I heard Rosie's voice from downstairs. "Mummy, Mummy, I'm coughing blood."

I froze. My breath caught in my throat and my heart began pounding. David was suddenly wide awake, and we rushed downstairs.

Rosie was standing by the door of the downstairs toilet. She was holding her hand cupped near her mouth. To my horror her hand was filled with blood.

"I'm scared, Mummy, Daddy, I'm really scared."

I tried to keep my voice steady, but I was shaking. David had rushed to the phone to call the ward.

"Don't worry, darling, it's probably just the warfarin levels are not quite right!"

Rosie just stared at her hand in horror. I felt sicker than I had ever felt in my life but tried to remain calm for her.

"They said if we are worried to take her in." David was fumbling to find the car keys.

I threw on some clothes then fastened her little red dressing gown and grabbed a plastic bowl from the kitchen and lots of tissues.

"David, we should call an ambulance, but if we do that, they will take her to Wexham and she needs to be at John Radcliffe as all her notes are there and they will know what to do."

"We will have to drive then," said David.

David carried Rosie to the car. I sat in the back seat beside her. Her skin felt clammy, and her eyes were wide. The dark shadows under them made them look sunken. I could see David's ashen face looking at Rosie in the rear-view mirror as he put his foot down and sped towards the M40 motorway and Oxford. She was saying it didn't hurt and did I think they would keep her in? I said I didn't know and then she became very quiet.

And then, "I can't breathe." Rosie was coughing and there were bloody tissues all over the back seat. I tried to put an arm round her to calm her, but she pushed me away. I felt helpless and unable to do anything. Mothers are supposed to protect their children. I was failing her and was powerless and the car was not going fast enough. David's foot was down, but it felt as though the world was standing still and we were trapped, unable to help our child.

At the end of the M40, we passed all the familiar landmarks. By the time we drove past McDonald's and through the streets of Headington towards the all too familiar grey walls of the hospital, Rosie was unable to breathe. She was gasping, "I need oxygen." She was clearly terrified and panicking.

David pulled up outside the hospital doors. I was running towards them, shouting that we needed a wheelchair. I grabbed one which was parked just inside the entrance and managed to get Rosie into it and started pushing the wheelchair towards the building, but the wheels would not go straight. A porter grabbed the chair and started running to the lift to the children's ward on the fourth floor. My mouth was dry. "Ward 4B. Just hurry, please."

The ward was so quiet. It was Bank Holiday Monday and most of the children who were well enough had gone home for the break. The nurse on duty stared dumbfounded as she saw us stumble through the entrance to the ward. I wondered why she was just standing there, but it was clear she was shocked. Another nurse took over, wheeling her to a bed at the far side of the bay.

"We must get a line in. Rosie is losing so much fluid."

"What, with no magic cream?" Rosie was so frightened.

"No, I'm so sorry, Rosie, we just don't have time. You are going to have to be really brave. We need to fast bleep to PICU!"

I heard another of Rosie's nurses on the phone to the paediatric intensive care unit. I could see the urgency and worry on her face. "FAST BLEEP, NOW!" An intensive care doctor ran in. She was going down to PICU. Rosie had an oxygen mask on but was becoming very woozy from losing fluids.

"What's happening? I'm going to die," Rosie cried. "Just put me to sleep. It hurts."

Then she was taken downstairs. The bed was being wheeled very fast towards the lift. David and I followed the bed in disbelief, still not really taking in what was happening. When we reached PICU, we were ushered into the waiting room. A nurse said, "We must get some more lines in. We will get her settled, then you can see her."

I stared at the cream-coloured walls. They felt as though they were closing in, and I wanted to run away. David called my mum. We sat helpless on the black plastic seats, then paced the tiny room. This must be what hell is.

Mum arrived with Sam, then came Robin and a lot of friends who were asked to remain outside. We could hear Rosie shouting. Shirley, her favourite PICU nurse, came in. I was so relieved to see a face I recognised. Shirley said, "She's okay! You can hear her, so she's okay! You can go in now before we sedate her."

David couldn't face it, but that was okay as long as I was with her. He went down the corridor to phone his brothers. I left Sam, Robin, and Mum in the side room and went to her bed. She was lying on her side, looking calmer. She looked at me and tried to smile and I said, "Be brave. I love you to bits, Rosie. I'll see you when you wake up."

In her piping voice she simply said, "I love you too, Mummy, and tell Daddy and Ellie."

I kissed her and went back to the waiting room.

Suddenly there was a commotion and hospital staff were running past the door. I tried to look and to my horror could see a crowd of medics were around the bed. They were trying to ventilate her. Anne Thomson, Rosie's respiratory consultant, rushed straight past us. She was in trousers and a jumper, looking as though she had arrived straight from her gardening. Her eyes were fixed on the door of PICU. She must have known we were there, but she was running, her car keys clinking in her hand, and she didn't even look at us or maybe she couldn't. She disappeared into the room and the doors closed. My child was in there and we were stuck not knowing, hardly able to breathe in a world where time was standing still.

After what seemed an eternity, Anne Thomson appeared. This time she came straight to me. Visibly shaken and upset, she knelt and took my hand. Looking straight into my eyes, she said as steadily as she could, "It's horrible. I have never seen anything like it. I don't think she's going to make it!"

"PLEASE," I cried, "PLEASE, JUST DON'T LET HER DIE. DON'T LET HER DIE, PLEASE GOD DON'T LET HER DIE!"

David sat in silence. He couldn't speak. He couldn't hold me, and I couldn't hold him. This pain and fear paralysed us both.

At that moment our world came crashing down. All that we had believed, all the happiness and joy we had ever known, belonged to another lifetime.

Mum clung to me. "It'll be alright, Carolyn. Listen to me. It will be alright," she kept saying. But in that moment the bottom had just fallen out of our beautiful world.

Mum, who always had an answer and a pragmatic solution for everything, was as powerless to change it as we were.

Someone brought Ellie to us, but I didn't know what to say to her. Her eyes were wide with terror, and she was crying. "Is she going to die? I don't want her to die." How in the hell could I tell my stricken oldest child who was only fourteen that her little sister was dying? How could I answer her truthfully when I could not even comprehend it myself? How could I make this nightmare go away? How could I wake up? How could I protect Ellie and retain some measure of composure and dignity when all that came out when I tried to speak was a strange sort of silent scream which stuck in my throat and made me wretch?

"She's arrested." I heard those words *cardiac arrest* as though I was watching from outside my body, witnessing someone else's story. I was so removed from the stark, terrible reality of the situation at that point that it was as though I was watching myself acting a role in a TV hospital drama. I watched the person who I know was me as Shirley led her to the end of the bed. I watched myself through the wrong end of a telescope, staring in utter disbelief. They were pumping her chest. I could hear counting. I saw Rosie's swollen face. Her eyes were open, staring upwards and unseeing.

I couldn't watch anymore. Shirley led me back to the family in the small side room.

Anne Thomson appeared. "She is seriously ill, on maximum ventilation, but she is alive and the next twenty-four hours will be crucial." With those words I landed back in my body and experienced my first panic attack. Everything was swimming around me, and I couldn't breathe or walk.

I remember being taken down to casualty. "Don't tell Mum. She'll just worry," I kept saying. I was given oxygen and then Shirley appeared and stayed with me. Her presence was a lifesaver. I kept thanking her and saying, "Please don't leave me." She said she was there for us for as long as we needed her. I felt so grateful to Shirley.

For the next few hours, all I can remember is leaning heavily on Shirley and being made to breathe into a brown paper bag.

When David and I were eventually able to see Rosie, her beautiful face was hardly recognisable. Machines were bleeping. Monitors and wires were everywhere, and an ugly, long grey tube was coming out of her mouth. They explained what they all were, but we didn't take much in.

Everyone eventually went home because they were totally exhausted and there was nothing more they could do. Ellie went back with my sister Sam. The hospital was no place for her, and she needed to be removed and taken care of. David and I stayed at the hospital.

We were shown into a parents' bedroom. It was one which was put aside for emergencies and for parents with children in intensive care. The room was horrible and stuffy with no windows, and we slept on bunk beds. There was plastic under the sheets on the beds. Every time we turned over, the plastic sheet crackled and rucked up. I will never forget the claustrophobia, the heat, and the smell of that room. We had no overnight clothes, but I think someone had found us some wash things and toothbrushes.

We stumbled down to PICU several times in the night. The report from the nurses at her bedside were the same each time. Rosie was "stable, serious, and stable!" I convinced myself that stable was a good sign and that she would be alright. David agreed that if she was stable, there was hope. She could improve. Miracles could happen.

Next day everyone treated us gently. The specialist on duty told us there was a chance of brain damage. She explained that when a child arrests for so long, it is almost definite that there would be some damage. Some children suffer mild damage and can return to school after six months. For others it can be more serious.

The rest of that week, we stumbled through in shock, disbelief, and pain.

I had never experienced anything like the cold, deadly, and terrifying horror as we somehow functioned on autopilot. Ellie, David, Mum, and I would visit. Days and nights merged into a never-ending limbo as we waited, hoped, and prayed for a sign of improvement.

Ellie sat with Rosie for hours each day, read her stories, and played tapes of one of her favourite musicals, *Honk*. She talked to her for ages, brushed her hair gently, and cleaned her teeth with a pink foam swab thing on a stick. I have no idea how Ellie coped with it, but her strength was extraordinary. Rosie would open her eyes and stare but without seeing. I would convince myself that she was hearing. "Squeeze my hand if you understand," I said.

We hoped and hoped, but hope was gradually fading. Her blood pressure kept shooting sky high and although they had reduced the sedation, there was still no response. The nurses were cagey and non-committal, so we kept hoping.

Six days passed and we began going home for a few hours and even slept a night or two at home because we were unable to do anything and there was nowhere to sleep at the hospital as they needed the room for other parents.

They wanted to do a brain trace, but Rosie was not well enough, so we dragged ourselves through the weekend. I was dosed up on diazepam, needing to block out the terror. On Monday it was one whole week since she had said, "I love you too, Mummy, and tell Daddy and Ellie."

That day Rosie's condition deteriorated.

On Tuesday we were told she would never be the Rosie we knew and loved. Anne Thomson said to us, "You know there are some things worse than death." I began to comprehend the undeniable reality of what she was saying.

On Wednesday, May 14th, nine days after our arrival on the unit, one of the doctors ushered us into a side room. We held our breath. Time seemed to stand still. She was grave and explained that Rosie was in a vegetative condition. There was nothing left. Whether they left the ventilator in for another day would make no difference.

She was brain stem dead!

The doctor said to us gently, "If I were you, I would allow her to die a dignified death. We will take the tube out and move her to a quiet room where you can be with her. It can take a few hours."

The tears were falling unchecked. We had no choice. David called the family. They all came.

We waited until she was settled.

They had moved her to a quiet little room next to the ward.

Our daughter was lying on her side, covered in a sheet. The tubes were gone. Her brown hair was spread out on a small pillow. She looked like a fragile sleeping beauty, but this princess would never be woken by a kiss.

I lay with her on the bed; I cuddled and talked to her. People came and went. They seemed like shadows. I remember the hushed voices and the tears. So many tears. David came in and out. His heart was breaking. He was unable to stay all the time and that was his way, but I couldn't leave my daughter. I had no recollection of the time.

And then she was gone.

Silence.

I heard Rosie in my head. She was swinging higher and higher on her swing.

"DON'T LIMIT MY LIFE. I DON'T WANT TO BE LIMITED IN ANY WAY."

Now she had no limits.

On that day, May 14th, 2003, we had no option but to face the terrible fact that our younger daughter was gone. I am not sure how long we laid with her or how we prised ourselves away for the last time before being led out of the intensive care unit.

The long sterile corridor was like a passage into a strange, new, unfamiliar world. It was a world I no longer recognised nor wished to be a part of.

We were led to a different part of the hospital, into a room labelled *Bereavement Services*. The new alien word *bereavement* entered my consciousness for the first time. What was this word?

I have no recollection of who showed us the way, but we found ourselves on two blue plastic stacking chairs in a small colourless room, staring blankly at a woman who handed us a weak cup of tea and introduced herself as bereavement support.

She was holding a leaflet called *How to register the death of a child*. I could see her mouth moving but couldn't process what she was saying. It must be for someone else. She put this on the top of a pile of other leaflets and handed it to me as if those leaflets contained all the information that we needed to carry us through the death of our precious child. Her hands were cold, and her handshake felt limp as she said that she was sorry. There isn't anything appropriate to say to shattered and devastated parents at such a tragedy of this magnitude, so perhaps that was all she could say at that moment.

As she showed us the door, I could hear her mumbling something about driving safely. We stumbled back along the corridor and out into the hospital car park, where I collapsed into the passenger seat next to a bewildered David.

We did not have a clue how to survive the catastrophe which had just befallen us. Our world had changed forever and how in the hell was this pile of paper going to be any use at all with the pain we were feeling at that time? How were we to look after Ellie and how were the family to survive in this world when Rosie was no longer in it?

David was silent. The car almost drove itself along the main road through Headington, past the odd-looking terraced house down one of the side roads, the one with the large shark sticking out of the roof which Rosie and Ellie had always found so amusing, and past the big McDonald's on the corner where we had often stopped to get Rosie a chicken nugget Happy Meal in an attempt to get her to eat, and then somehow we were on the M40 and driving back towards Maidenhead and the rest of our lives.

Mounded
May 14th, 2003

The bereavement lady advised us to stop at the registry office on the way home to register the death. We found the building and went through the procedure in a state of shock and disbelief. Leaving the registry office with the envelope stating the time place and reason of death, we somehow found our way home.

We were afraid to go back into the house. I couldn't face entering our home. Rosie's things were still as they were, her black and yellow theatre school bag she had packed was by the front door and filled with schoolbooks, leotards, and dance shoes for when she went back to school. Everything was in place ready for her to continue her life.

Mum suggested we go to her house, to my old bedroom at Redroofs, so we stopped there.

Her pretty garden was springing into life with daffodils and buds on the trees. There was a soft scent of lilac and at the end of the garden, a row of pink and white magnolias were beginning to bloom. I felt pure anger that here was new growth when our daughter's life was snuffed out so cruelly. It was all wrong.

It was devastating to witness Mum crumbling. My mother, who always said everything would be okay, who I always believed could fix anything, was unable to mend this. For the first time my rock and pillar of strength was broken and rendered incapable, just as we were. But then in an extraordinary effort to keep things together, she went into a frantic coping mode. Maybe it was her Jewish matriarchal genes kicking in, but she cooked salmon, new potatoes, and chicken soup to sustain us even though I couldn't eat. To this day poached salmon conjures up painful memories of those few days and I still struggle to eat it.

In his gentle and unassuming manner, Sam's partner Phil took over the funeral arrangements because we were grief-stricken, unable to think straight, let alone organise an impossible and unbelievable farewell.

My mother began tapping into the computer. She was writing a piece for the funeral. I could see she referred to a word coined by Rosie which she used many times when she felt overworked, overloaded, even when she was asked to carry a pile of toys upstairs.

"I'm mounded," Rosie used to say. And Mum wrote of being *mounded* by grief. It was a fitting adjective for how we all felt.

That same day Mum said that she had woken up during the night hearing crying. Then she realised it was herself. Mum never cries – at least not in public.

Whilst funeral arrangements were being made, I huddled on her green wicker sofa in the kitchen, legs drawn tight to my chest, head down, foetal and rocking.

I couldn't stop rocking and rocking and rocking.

Waking up in my old bed in the mornings, there were a few seconds of nothingness as I blinked my eyes open, then a tidal wave of fear and unbearable cold would wash over me, followed by the freezing icy darkness of reality. We would drag ourselves out of bed and dress to face another day. The simplest acts were now so difficult. Even brushing my teeth made me wretch.

Sam, as a teacher in our school, had the grim job of breaking the news to Rosie's friends and to all the pupils and teachers. She forced herself to hold a special assembly where all the children and staff were overcome with tears of grief. School lessons were cancelled, and each child set about writing memories of their friend. Some penned poems, others made pictures. I am not sure how she was able to hold it together, but somehow she did.

At Mum's house there were non-stop phone calls, family visits, lists drawn up of who to notify regarding the funeral. The news spread on the grapevine, and letters of sympathy arrived from friends, family, and parents of our school pupils. Through all of this I curled up in the corner of a sofa and rocked, further and further removed from reality.

We received a visit from Rabbi Jonathan Romain from Maidenhead synagogue. This kind man gave me a book called *When Bad Things*

Happen to Good People. His visit seemed to help Mum and I was grateful to him for trying to say the right thing. I was impressed that he wasn't offering that all too familiar and hackneyed line, *Well, God needed her more*, or overwhelming us with prayers for the dead, but even he could not change anything.

My rocking was brought to a sudden and abrupt end less than forty-eight hours after Rosie's passing. David was in Mum's kitchen. I was in my foetal position, eyes tight shut, trying to block out the world and the actual physical pain. He was leaning against the billiard table when he complained of pains in his chest. These grew worse over the next few hours and a call to the paramedics suggested he was suffering a possible heart attack. Mum said, "You are going to have to pull yourself together, Carolyn. We need to call an ambulance!"

I was jolted into autopilot and into the present as an ambulance pulled up outside the house. They took him to the ambulance, where the paramedics began pumping him with the same drugs Rosie had been given. I had a sinister and scary wave of déjà vu as they administered heparin and oxygen, before he was taken to Wexham Park, then transferred to the Brompton hospital in London where he was fitted with a stent and put on statins to regulate his heart.

His brother Colin and my sister-in-law Niki drove me up the M4 to see him. They were so gentle and kind, trying to do what they could to help.

We found him lying in a hospital bed in a ward full of heart patients. He was motionless and staring at the ceiling. He flatly said that he wanted to go and be with Rosie and didn't want to live anymore. I told him harshly not to be so bloody selfish and that he must get better because he had Ellie and me and he was not going to take the coward's way out. For the first time David did as he was told and recovered sufficiently from the operation to be discharged a day before the funeral.

Out of us all, Ellie, our fourteen-year-old, was the only one who appeared to be functioning. She had returned to school and seemed to put her grief for her beloved sister into a place where she did not have to confront it. How she managed I will never know, but she showed extraordinary strength and resilience at that time.

Laura was such a good best friend to her and had the idea of creating *Memories of Rosie*, a website where Rosie's friends and family could share memories and write about their feelings. Special friends stepped up to support Ellie. They took her out and into their homes for some respite. I felt hopeless and very guilty about being unable to help Ellie. I was rendered totally incapable of looking after her. After those awful early days, I learnt that teenagers and young people often compartmentalise their grief when they are bereaved, and it's often many years later that pain and grief surfaces.

We summoned up the courage to ask Rosie's nurse Shirley to take on the difficult task of plaiting Rosie's hair for the funeral. I am not sure how Shirley managed to do this for us. It was a massive thing to ask her to visit Rosie in the hospital mortuary, but she readily agreed and even said she was honoured to have been asked. They had experienced good and bad times in hospital and their mutual interest in all things theatrical enabled her and Rosie to share a lot of banter. Knowing Rosie and dealing with her and us through this catastrophic tragedy changed everything for her. She had a special relationship with our daughter while she nursed her over those last few months.

By the time David arrived home, everything for the funeral was arranged and ready for the final farewell to our little girl. Somehow we had survived nine whole days and nights.

Once Upon a December
May 23rd, 2003

Dosed up on diazepam, I only remember the funeral in flashes. There were more than 500 people present, and I recall a sea of faces and my dear cousins sobbing at the entrance.

I stared at the coffin in light wood and the flowers, just as they had been in my head that day in the hospital. The vision of the funeral and the detail was exactly as I had foreseen. That premonition in minutest detail had come true and we were living it.

We took our places in the crematorium. I could see Machiel on the platform, playing the song *Once Upon a December*. My mind wandered briefly back to just a year ago. A normal day in our theatre school. Rosie glowing, smiling, and excited as she sang.

Dancing bears,
Painted wings,
Things I almost remember,
And a song someone sings
Once upon a December.

I was reliving Rosie's ten-year-old voice, pure and sweet, as the audience of children in her class listened to her rendition from *Anastasia*.

Rosie had chosen the song and had practised hard for several days for this informal presentation, singing in the kitchen, in the car, in her bedroom, and now at the performance. Being her proud mummy, I mouthed the words as she sang.

Someone holds me safe and warm,
Horses prance through a silver storm.
Figures dancing gracefully across my memory.

A year later here I sat in a hard pew, my whole being frozen in agony as I stared at Machiel on the platform of the crematorium. His hands were trembling, and tears were falling unchecked on the keyboard. He was supposed to be singing the lyrics, but nothing came out. His fingers somehow managed to play the tune, but he kept repeating the same line of music over and over. He was trying not to look in my direction and to do his best to be there for me and to pay his respects to Rosie.

She was so much still there, but of course she was not there.

My daughter would never sing again. Well, not in the truest sense anyway.

I silently mouthed the words as I heard her voice in my head.

Far away,
Long ago,
Glowing dim as an ember,
Things my heart used to know,
Things it yearns to remember.
And a song someone sings
Once upon a December.

In the afternoon our friends transferred the mountain of flowers from the crematorium to our Novello Theatre in Ascot and the auditorium was packed with friends and close family. The 160-seat Pollock's-style theatre had been Rosie's playroom throughout her life. Now it seemed appropriate that this was where her final performance should be.

Her little school friends sat on the stage sobbing and reading poems and pieces they had written.

Rosie's cousins looked so bewildered as they clung to each other and said farewell. There were now nine cousins instead of ten. One small girl missing, forever leaving one gaping hole which could never be filled. Friends and family were all still in deep shock. I realised that if we were to survive at all, then something positive must come out of this horror.

I was wearing a brightly coloured blazer because Rosie loved colour and was still in disbelief that this had happened to our chirpy, chatty daughter who was so full of life, love, rainbow stripes, and fun. How the hell were we to find a way forward and drag ourselves out of this black pit?

After the tribute we stood at the theatre entrance. It was surreal as our friends and family filed out of the auditorium almost in silence. They hung around for a while, offering what words they could to try to comfort us.

On that unreal afternoon I said to a friend but almost to myself, "I've decided I must create something for Rosie. Something that will last so that she will never be forgotten. I want to raise money for all those children she had been so concerned about during her time on ward 4B at the hospital."

As I shared this lightbulb moment, I looked up at the sky just above the theatre and saw the most incredible double rainbow I had ever seen, bright, huge, and immediately over the theatre roof. It wasn't even raining. It was as if Rosie was standing right beside me in her brightest rainbow-striped tights and whispering directions in my ear. She was telling me in no uncertain terms that she was still very much there and would make damn sure her wish was carried out.

"It's Rosie's Rainbow," I whispered. "That's it."

I found David. "She has chosen the name of her legacy. It's going to be Rosie's Rainbow Fund." And so, in that instant, it was all decided. It was as simple as that. There was no question. Rosie, in her usual forthright way, told us to get on with it. She always used to say, "Don't talk about it. DO it."

Now in my head I saw her sitting on that rainbow, perched right in the middle. Wearing her favourite stripy tights which seemed to merge with the stripes of the rainbow. Her legs swinging freely over the edge, her hair in two plaits just slightly askew. She was smiling down at us. It felt as though she was going to make sure we had a focus and that whatever it took we were going to survive this devastation.

Cold Bones
May 25th, 2003

Although it was late May and the weather was warming up, the days following the funeral felt black and icy cold. Each morning I awoke to a few seconds of numbness, followed by a feeling of drowning in a freezing tidal wave. This paralysed me. I had read about having cold bones. Now I understood what that meant. My bones were like ice. I couldn't get warm. I longed to be held, but there was little physical comfort from anyone.

David was locked in his own grief, but truthfully it was Rosie I needed to hold and no one else. The ache and longing for her became impossible. There were bad days and worse days and just occasionally some lighter days. These left me feeling guilty because I was not feeling the intensity of pain all the time. Also, I was afraid that if I was not experiencing stark piercing pain all the time, this meant I was forgetting Rosie or leaving her behind. However, when the pain returned, which it always did, it was so intense I thought I would die.

We moved back to our house. In some ways it was a relief, but the three of us faced a place which no longer felt like home. We were in a strange new existence. Everything we knew suddenly looked different, shadowy, sinister, and frightening. I could have been underwater, drowning or scrabbling around on a seabed in a dark world I no longer recognised. I experienced despair of the greatest magnitude, a depth of loneliness I had never felt before, and an unbearable longing to be reunited with my precious child. My single reason for getting through each day was to care for Ellie. She had lost her sister and her little soulmate.

Friends and family visited and tried to help. This brought some structure to the days and got me up each morning. They were kind and concerned, and for a month or so, the diary was full of endless lunches and coffees.

They did their best, but what could they say when there were no words? It was a question of getting through another day, but on many of these days, I could only concentrate on getting through an hour at a time or even sometimes a minute. Some friends couldn't deal with our grief. Maybe they were afraid of making me more upset or perhaps they just didn't know what to say.

On the flip side, there were people who became very much closer. Those who I had hardly known before, who were not afraid to open their arms to me and my family, were there to hold us up.

Looking into the future was just too frightening. I had no idea how to live without my beautiful younger daughter. How the hell could I live the rest of my life without her mischievous presence, without hearing her laughter, never being able to hold her again? I would clutch her little pink hat that she had worn so much and press it to my face to try to smell her hair. Over time the smell faded, which was almost impossible to cope with.

David had a desperate urge to enlarge a pile of photos of Rosie, so he took a huge envelope to a local picture framing shop and had a set of photos put in light wood frames and behind glass. After a while he began to spend an increasing amount of time at the gym. This became a daily obsession. I was glad that his health was improving, but he was never at home. When I came in, he went out. His evenings were spent taking his grief out on the gym equipment and his personal trainer.

Looking for support, I heard about a group called the Compassionate Friends. There was a helpline phone number. It was a dark afternoon in our empty house and, feeling desperate, I gathered the courage to call the number.

A lady at the other end of the line was kind and concerned. She explained that all the volunteers on the phone lines were bereaved parents themselves and so they understood what newly bereaved parents were going through. She introduced me to a website with a forum of bereaved mums and some dads. In those days before Facebook, this forum became a source of great comfort to me. The mums I met were in varying stages of grief. There were some newly bereaved and still in shock like me, and others that were years down the line. They offered coping mechanisms and a virtual shoulder to cry on, and most importantly they understood and at that stage became close friends.

We shared so much together, often in the middle of the night. Some had heart-rending stories of the death of more than one child, and the reasons for the deaths of their children ranged from sudden death to long-term illness, suicide, and murder. It was a weird way to forge friendships, but our bond was unquestionable.

We faced birthdays and anniversaries together and shared coping strategies. They came from a wide area, and none were local to me, but we were truly united in our grief, and I was indebted to my growing circle of online friends for this unwavering love and support when I felt incapable of even getting through another night.

One evening there was a knock at the front door. A lady stood on my doorstep. She was maybe sixty and still pretty. Her curly blonde hair framed a gentle face and light blue eyes.

"I have been told about you and the loss of your precious little girl. My name is Jenni Thomas and I have come to offer you support at this simply awful time."

Like Mary Poppins, Jenni came into our lives when we most needed her. I could only describe her as an earthly angel. In our now eerily quiet living room, she listened attentively to our story. She knew how to help me to articulate my feelings. I never had a problem unburdening. Women often find it helpful to talk and talk and talk. David found that very difficult, but she seemed to know how to coax him to speak a little. With her vast experience of how to be with grief-stricken parents, she knew just what to say. The support she gave us and the tools she gave me to cope with my grief were a lifesaver. This gracious lady was knowledgeable and caring beyond belief. She was the founder of the charity Child Bereavement Trust and over the years had supported and helped many hundreds of grieving families. The charity had grown, and Jenni had been awarded an OBE for her extraordinary work.

She invited us to attend a support group at their headquarters in

West Wycombe. David came to one but then declined to attend again as he found it too difficult. He was not able to articulate his feelings and was very uncomfortable. I went along to several of these sessions, which were difficult but helpful. I met more families who had suffered the loss of a child and again realised that there were so many bereaved parents out there, all dealing with the same nightmare. These sessions were invaluable and my admiration and trust in Jenni saw me through some very tough times. Jenni discussed post-traumatic stress disorder. She suggested that considering what we had been through, it would hardly be surprising if we were suffering from this too. She introduced me to an experienced bereavement counsellor. It had become apparent that I was not able to talk freely to my family about my loss. Mum would well up every time I mentioned Rosie. It made me feel awful to watch her grieve and over time we all hid our tears from each other.

Ellie couldn't deal with my heartache and her own pain and was often brittle and distant. On the positive side she immersed herself in composing songs on the piano. Together with Laura, she was able to write how she felt. They composed songs which were so moving, and which were Ellie's release at a time when she was unable to talk about her sister. Music had the ability to release emotion. It was good that at least music and song continued in our home even if the tunes were melancholy. They spent hours together at our piano or at Laura's house. Ellie played their latest songs, 'Does It Rain in Heaven?' and 'A Rainbow's Light'.

I had some amazing friends and shared a good deal with them, but there were some things which needed to be in a private place, so a counsellor was certainly what I needed.

More Loss
June 2003

Rosie's Golden Retriever Tessie had been staying with one of my dearest friends Candice in the long months that Rosie was in hospital. When she brought her home to us a few days after the funeral, Tessie was withdrawn, quiet, and clearly unwell. The vet was concerned, and we were referred to a specialist hospital for tests.

Just as we thought things could not get any worse, we were horrified to discover that Tessie's kidneys were failing and that our dog's prognosis at the age of just two years old was terminal with only six weeks to live. While we had been all consumed with Rosie's illness, our pet insurance had run out and we had to foot the bill ourselves. The vet did reduce it on compassionate grounds after I broke down, so we managed to pay, but it was still a lot of money!

After a few more weeks of desperately trying and failing to find a cure, we had to accept that Tessie's short life was over too. The vet came to the house. David was at work and Ellie at school, so Candice came to be with me. In the living room on her favourite blanket, I held her and stroked her and whispered, "It's okay, Tess, you can go and find Rosie now." The vet gave her an injection and then Tessie was gone too. I tried to make sense of it by thinking that Rosie needed her up there and that she had gone to be with her.

It was not the end of those terrible times. Rosie's little black and white cat Daisy disappeared a few weeks later. Despite posting desperate messages around the area, Daisy was never found. Had she gone to join Rosie too?

There was the immense issue hanging over us all of what to do with Rosie's ashes. We had chosen a cremation and therefore there was no grave. We were given a casket after the committal but had no idea what to do with it. We couldn't bear it in the house, so it stayed in the garage wrapped up. I felt awful that Rosie was there in a dark garage, but having her in the house was too painful.

We finally decided to put the casket in our garden. David and his brothers dug a hole right in the middle of our lawn, placed the box in it, and planted a magnolia tree. It was the purple Rosie loved. One of her favourite colours and as vivid as her personality. He said Rosie liked to be centre stage, so there it was. Every time we looked out of the window, it was the first thing we saw. The tree grew, but the pain of looking at it and knowing that was all that was left of our darling Rosie grew too.

We all found writing to be a useful means of expressing grief. Laura's *Memories of Rosie* website contained a growing pile of daily postings, writings, musings, and a lot of poems. Many of our friends and family posted and responded to postings with genuine love and affection. It provided an outlet and a common place to share grief.

As the days passed my concern for Ellie increased. Although her strength through the tragedy had been remarkable, she was experiencing inconceivable loneliness. One evening I went into her bedroom. She was under her duvet hunched up, miserable, and looking so lost. "Mummy, come and sit on the bed." She sat up and her green eyes were filled with tears. I was aching for her while she tried to find the words.

"When will it stop hurting like this?" As usual I had no answer but tried to come up with something helpful. It came out sounding inappropriate and futile. I was so afraid of saying the wrong thing, but at that moment nothing was the right thing.

"I don't know, Ellie. But I have been told that although we will always be sad, it does become easier. You miss her so much, don't you?"

She nodded and lay back on her pillows.

"There is something worse than this," she whispered.

"What's that?"

I waited and then she said, "When Rosie was in a vegetative state, that was worse."

I said, "Yes, but at least we had her to hold, and we could touch her."

"Yes," she said, "but then, although we had her body, we didn't have her spirit. It just wasn't there. Now we have her spirit but no body!"

I could only utter, "Yes, I guess so." I was completely taken aback at the statement from my bereft fourteen-year-old. She put her arms round me and buried her head in my shoulder as I felt the trickle of her tears down my neck. Grabbing a box of Kleenex, I just held her until her sobs quietened and then subsided as she fell asleep.

The next morning we drove to Asda. We saw other mums in the store with their kids. They were just being ordinary, but I couldn't look at them.

Ellie and I found the children's clothes rail. There were rows of stripy tee shirts. Had Rosie been there I would have bought one.

I remembered a trip to that store a few months earlier. Rosie was in hospital and David was looking after her that afternoon. I had gone home for a few hours. I had loaded the washing machine and cleared up a bit. Then I collected Mum and Ellie, and we were on our way back towards John Radcliffe Hospital. Before we hit the M40, we stopped off en route to shop. That day Rosie had been quite full of beans, and she was happy spending a few hours of quality time with her daddy. Mum, Ellie, and I bought loads of stuff for Rosie to cheer her up. We were almost manic on that trip. It had always been my greatest pleasure, children's clothes shopping, and that day we seemed to want to buy Rosie everything on the shelf and we emerged with Asda bags full of bright cheap clothes, and some plastic plates with colourful pictures on to try to tempt her to eat more.

I knew she would look great in the new clothes, even though I had to buy age seven to eight as she had become so thin. I also knew how she would really appreciate everything she received. All through her life she had never asked for anything and that made the giving so easy. She used to say, "Mummy, I don't need anything. Buy something for Ellie. Save your money."

At the checkout Ellie bought some chewy strawberry sweets and some of those white chocolate buttons with hundreds and thousands on, the sort which Rosie liked.

Ellie had to try to come to terms with the impossible fact that normal times hanging out with her sister were over. Over the years my daughters would love to sit together on the old red check tablecloth on our living room floor, watching *The Simpsons* and eating bowls of pasta Bolognese. There used to be hours and days spent playing with their collection of Beanie Babies, who all had names and occupations, and the stuffed toys had their own suitcase with breathing holes punched in the side so they could travel with the children on holidays as Rosie was concerned they wouldn't be able to breathe if the suitcase was locked.

Our girls were close in so many ways. There used to be silly arguments about all the normal sisterly things. But now Ellie stopped sitting on the floor. The Beanies were put away into a plastic box in the playroom cupboard. There were no breathing holes in that box which seemed obsolete now. It seemed that she had been forced to grow up overnight. My elder daughter now stared silently at the TV or spent hours playing sad tunes on the piano. She stopped eating pasta Bolognese. She told me the smell made her feel sick.

Ellie returned to school at the beginning of June, just a week after the funeral. Approaching her GCSE years with tenacity and quiet strength, she somehow accessed the reserves to just get on with it. I had no idea how she managed, particularly since Rosie had also been a pupil at our school and she had to face going back without her. I was nowhere near ready to return to work at the school. Rosie had been such a strong presence there. Now there was an empty space in the dance class line and an empty desk in her classroom. No one felt they could sit in Rosie's place.

Compartmentalising her grief as though she had locked it away into a box and sealed it, her friends rallied round for her, and she spent a lot of time with Laura. Oddly she was at her most musically creative at that time and her compositions were endless.

Rosie's Bench
July 2003

David decided to buy a memorial bench for Rosie's school friends. Painstakingly he painted the bench in vivid rainbow-coloured gloss paint and had a gold plaque engraved and fixed to the centre of the back of the bench. This read *Rosie's Rainbow Bench*. He delivered it to our school garden.

We arranged a little dedication ceremony on the last day of the school term. This was another difficult day that we needed to face. Although he had painted the bench with a great deal of patience and pride, David didn't go. He was too upset. So, Ellie, Mum, and I took the whole school out in the garden and gathered round the seat with Rosie's friends, the rest of the pupils, and all the staff.

The day was stiflingly hot and there was no wind at all. That day the stillness felt odd, and I could not work out why. Rosie's little friend stood by the bench, clutching a sheet of paper in her hand on which she had written a poem that she began to read aloud. As she started the poem, a warm wind blew up almost out of nowhere, rustling the paper until it blew out of her hand and onto the grass. The oddest thing was that it didn't feel like wind. It was strange and unearthly, and rustled the branches of the tree which was next to us. I could hear music in the branches which sounded like wind chimes. The noise of the wind became so loud that the head teacher had to ask the child who was reading to speak much louder because no one could hear the words. It was as though Rosie had blown up this wind and was blowing the kids' voices in the wrong direction. I thought I was imagining it and convinced myself that it was my sensitive head state.

As soon as the children left, the wind ceased completely, and everything suddenly went still. It was the strangest experience and one which has not happened since.

I asked Mum later that afternoon if she had noticed anything and she said, "Yes, I did. It was that wind." She agreed it had been uncanny.

I relayed this to Sam later. Oddly she said that at exactly that time, Rowan and Sasha were in their kitchen at home and had been talking to each other about Rosie. Rowan had said, "How will Rosie blow out candles on her birthday cake?" and Sasha had answered, "The wind will blow them out!"

The next day I went into school. From one of the classrooms upstairs, I could see Rosie's friends. They were clamouring to sit on her bench. There was laughter. I remember my hands against the window, my forehead on the glass, my breath on the window, my eyes red and my throat dry. Rosie's maths teacher was the only one who noticed I was there and the only one to acknowledge my grief. It was with just a couple of words, but it was something, and it was enough for me in that briefest moment as I watched Rosie's friends begin to learn to live without her.

A year before Rosie became ill, we had bought The Philberds, a large, lofty white house sitting in an acre of land on the Ascot Road in Holyport. It was not a pretty building, but David and I had been impressed with the size of the house with huge high-ceilinged rooms on three floors. The idea was that David would carry out an extensive renovation on the house. I had a picture in my mind of how impressive and smart it could look. David suggested that we should sell our present house and live in a mobile home onsite while he carried out the massive amount of work. I couldn't face the idea of living in a mobile home. Renovations always take longer than planned, so we agreed that we would stay in our old home until the new house was ready.

Taking the girls to view their future home, we tried to imagine a finished house. Ellie was excited by the potential of the property and was busy visualising which of the rooms would be hers, but Rosie made it no secret that she despised the feel of the place. With one look of disgust, she said, "I am *not* moving in here. I hate it. It's so spooky and weird. If you do move in, then I'm going to go and live at Grandma's."

I tried to explain how stunning it would look when the renovations were complete, but she was adamant that it did not feel right. Rosie liked orderly, bright, cosy little houses rather like her doll's house, which she adored and which she and I spent many months furnishing with countless trips to the doll's house collectors' shop in Twyford. Rosie and I spent hours in the shop while she carefully chose a miniature family, teeny plates of food and cutlery, tables, beds, tiny plant pots, and chairs. She used to like its neatness and she enjoyed her tidy little doll's house world which was arranged just to her liking.

By spring 2002 we were no nearer to starting renovations and the cold, gloomy white house sat empty. Realising that Rosie was probably right as usual, we decided to put The Philberds back on the market. For many months there was a *for sale* sign outside, but no one wanted to buy it. We had made a big mistake. We should have listened to Rosie. She was the smallest and youngest in our family but certainly the wisest. Later that year when Rosie became ill, we took it off the market.

Early July, two months after we lost Rosie, I was invited to have coffee with a kind lady who lived locally and who had lost two children. We were sharing our sad stories when David telephoned.

"Don't panic, but the house is on fire! I'm just on my way down there. You need to come."

The lady stared at me shocked as I excused myself from the meeting, apologetically trying to explain although I felt like laughing hysterically. "I've just had a call from my husband to say the house is on fire. It's okay. It's only a house, just bricks, and Rosie hated it anyway!"

I drove straight to the house and on my arrival was greeted by thirty-five firefighters battling to bring the massive flames under control. There was a lot of smoke and we stood there staring at the carnage, wondering what on earth had happened. It turned out that a bunch of local ten-year-old kids had been using the empty house as a den and had been playing with matches in one of the upstairs bathrooms. They accidentally set the curtains alight, and the house had gone up in flames. They managed to get out and were lucky to escape unharmed as they could have been killed, but the house was burnt to the ground.

When we revisited the site next morning, all that was left was part of a staircase. The rest of the house was a blackened burnt-out shell of a building with a horrible smoky stench after being doused with thousands of gallons of water. What we found upon closer examination freaked us out. In one of the remaining rooms, we saw a crucifix made of twigs stuck to the wall. All around the crucifix were dark red rose petals. The sight made us shiver. Why rose petals? Or were they *Rosie* petals!

The downstairs toilet had been wallpapered by the previous owners with manuscript sheet music of old songs. The paper was largely burnt away, but what remained still glued to the wrecked wall were three sheets of scrappy brown manuscript bearing the titles of three songs. We read them in disbelief: 'Never Forget', 'Missing You', and 'This Nearly Was Mine'. "Oh my God, look, David, OH my God." Then we started to laugh uncontrollably. "Well, Rosie managed to get rid of the damned thing and good riddance."

We eventually sold the land to a developer.

Thank you, Rosie.

One evening, feeling totally wretched, I went upstairs to Rosie's bedroom. It was becoming increasingly difficult to go in there at all.

I stood in her room for some time. Her bed was still made up with the sunshine yellow duvet cover with coloured animals on it. Her favourite lime green Beanie cat was where she had left it on the pillow. Ornaments and a few nick-nacks were still on her white chest of drawers. She had put a few random stickers with yellow smiley faces and pink hearts on the knobs. They had begun to peel off round the edges now. Her black and yellow school blazer was hanging on the door, her name tape sewn in the collar and a scrunched-up tissue still in the pocket with a couple of hair pins.

Her clothes were still in the drawers. Top drawer socks and underwear, middle drawer pyjamas, where they had been on that day when life changed forever and when hers abruptly stopped. The bottom drawer contained notebooks, felt tips, photos, and general little girls' stuff.

For some reason I ran my hand under her chest of drawers. Feeling something under there, I pulled out some pages of her little secret diary given to her the previous Christmas. I had no clue as to why she had torn them out, but she had scrunched them up and must have shoved them under the drawers. Sitting on her bed, I smoothed the crumpled pages.

In her best handwriting she had written:

Name – Rosie Mayling
Age – 11
Eyes – Green
Favourite food – watermelon and crispy duck
Favourite book – The Dolls House
Favourite Colour – Red
Favourite group/boyband – none
Favourite shop – M and S
Hobbies and interests – Acting, Singing
Friends I trust with secrets – Emma, Sophie, Hayley
My secret worries and fears – Erak. [Iraq]
My ambitions – to love and be loved.
The kind of person I want to become – a caring and loving person
My role models – My Mum and Dad
My biggest secret – I want to see into the future and let there be love

Had she somehow intended that I find them? That little crumpled scrap of comfort helped me through the night.

Gulls, Waves, Tears
August 2003

Just ten weeks had passed since the funeral. We were all worn out. Dee suggested that a break would do us good and she kindly invited us to Brittany for a week to stay in her sister's flat with her and the children.

David wasn't keen. "How can we go on holiday ten weeks after we have lost our child?"

I tried to reason with him. "It's not a holiday. It's some time to try to heal and it will be comfortable to be in the company of such close friends and it will be so good for Ellie to be with Lucy and Laura."

"I'm so tired of grieving," David said with a sigh. Ellie agreed it was a good idea, so the three of us caught the ferry to France.

Dee was so kind and patient, but it was impossible for us to relax. The comfortable apartment in Sables d'Or on the Brittany coast was just a stone's throw from a wide sandy beach and we were in the company of dear friends who knew and loved Rosie and with whom we didn't have to pretend. Ellie was unsettled and snappy, even with her best friend Laura.

David did have a couple of good fishing trips. We tried hard to be pleasant company.

Sometimes I could not manage to keep up the brave face and wandered alone up and down the beach in the evenings. Seeing little pigtailed girls in stripy tee shirts and baseball caps playing in the sand brought acute physical pain. Grateful for the noise of the waves, I sobbed. It seemed a cathartic thing to do and somehow release some tension. I found a stick and drew her name into the sand, *ROSIE*. Then of course the waves washed it away. It became a competition between me, the waves, and the gulls as to who could cry the loudest.

Dee was so sad too. All the girls had been at school together and had been in our lives since Ellie and Laura became dancing partners at the age of five, and Dee and I had become such firm friends over the years. She had watched Rosie grow from a toddler to a chatty, bright, interesting little girl and Dee and I had spent a memorable trip with all four of our girls staying in the same French village only a year before.

The little quartet had spent their days not playing on the beach but inventing a wickedly funny musical review with outrageous but hilarious impersonations of the school staff. They had written lyrics and an entire script and had enthusiastically performed for Dee's friend, who was passing through Sables d'Or and had made a surprise visit. Instead of a relaxing evening, the poor lady was forced to watch and applaud this hour-long wicked parody. Rosie was hysterically funny.

Those happy memories made a return trip to the sleepy little Brittany village very difficult. Despite everything we were rested, the sea air was restorative, and the break did help.

On the way home on the ferry, Ellie and I decided that a new puppy would be a great focus and a positive distraction, so we spent some hours together writing down possible names for the new dog.

After our trip the next few days felt a little lighter. Our new Golden Retriever pup arrived shortly after. Alfie was a round bundle of golden fur and cuteness with large blonde paws. He didn't take the pain away, but he was life-affirming, and his carefree puppy antics kept us in the present. Ellie was enchanted with him, and I hoped he would be become as much her dog as Tessie had been Rosie's.

It was as though I had grown a mask. Behind the mask was the loss and hopelessness, the death of Rosie and the death of most of me. Wearing this mask most of the time, I laughed, joked, and somehow managed to appear to cope with normal everyday stuff on autopilot. This must be what the textbooks said about *learning to deal with it*. There was a realisation that the pain was not going to go away anytime soon, but oddly, although we were just weeks after our loss, we were already learning to hide it. I chose to do my best because that was what Rosie would have wanted and imagined how she would fret if she saw that her death had broken us all, and how happy she would be to know that we were surviving. I was, however, aware that this was just an act and while it was possible to kid everyone else, the truth was that inside

I felt I had died too.

In my grief I was beginning to discover more about a parallel world. I had developed a fascination for spiritual things even as far back as messing about with a Ouija board and tarot cards at boarding school, but it always frightened me.

Machiel had been gentle and supportive since that day at the cremation. We began to spend a lot of time together and I found solace as he began to tell me about his own spiritual beliefs. He has an absolute belief that there is an afterlife where Rosie now exists. Her soul continues and she is watching over us. He introduced me to *Conversations with God*, a series of books by Neale Donald Walsch. I read them all with an obsessive and urgent need to know that she existed – even in another dimension – and one day I would see her again.

Soon I was devouring every book relating to children in spirit and how they let us know they are with us. Each one backed up this theory and brought much comfort.

Machiel would come to our house with his partner Martin, who was not a believer but accepted that Machiel was teaching me. Machiel would sit at the piano, we would all gather around, and the house would fill with music and song. Ellie and I would invite other musical friends to join these soirées.

Jayne had the voice of a nightingale. As a seven-year-old with dimples and a cherubic face, she had been cast as the very first little Cosette in the opening London production of *Les Misérables* and had been runner up in ITV's *Opportunity Knocks* and then years later, as an adult professional, went on to play the role of grown-up Cosette. Machiel would often accompany Jayne on the piano at some of her gigs.

The three of us would eat at a curry house in Marlow and spent hours discussing our views on the spirit world and the afterlife, which was now my obsession. I loved our evenings together. Machiel called us the Three Musketeers. The two of them helped me through some tough evenings and their laughter and banter was uplifting.

Jodie, one of this group of slightly madcap creatives, had taken Ellie under her wing, and we welcomed her too along with her partner Scott. Jodie and Scott were regular cast members in the Novello shows, where Jodie and Rosie had developed a strong connection. She was outgoing with a broad Nottingham accent and a vocal belt as big as her zany personality. Her ability to regress to big kid and her gregarious nature meant Rosie had a willing ally and she would mischievously encourage Rosie's backstage antics. Machiel was a prolific and successful composer. He released various albums of hit songs in his native South Africa. He would play his own compositions. Then we would move on to sing all the musical theatre favourites. When there was music, I felt closer to Rosie.

One evening Jodie disclosed to me that she had *seen* Rosie at the theatre. She had not only felt her presence, but she had also seen her on several occasions.

"I gave Rosie a special wave last night in the spot that I always see her."

"Er, what do you mean?" I stammered.

"I waved to her at the end of the show. I went back to the dressing room and told the others, and I think they were quite shocked."

"Where?"

"Above the lighting box in the left spotlight. It was one of my visions I keep getting. She was smiling with all her hair down. It only lasted for a split sec, but it was nice. She waved though. It was just like I was looking in a mirror and Rosie was inside looking back, smiling and waving back to me as I went offstage. Ellie was singing onstage at the time. It felt real, but it was very quick, so not sure for definite."

"That's so lovely. Did she look okay?"

"Oh, she looked very happy and was laughing – and yes, she just looked exactly like Rosie. She had a pink top with a BIG butterfly on it, but I could only see her head and shoulders... and lots of hair!"

"I wish I had seen it. Jodie, are you just saying that?"

"Of course not. I promise," she added. "I wasn't gonna tell you."

"You must tell me. Every time, please. Have there been other times you haven't told me?"

"Other times it felt like imagination, but last night it didn't, if that makes sense?"

Ellie had been at Jodie's house. They were on the computer looking at the *Memories of Rosie* website. The sun was streaming in through the window. Jodie was messing about on the computer to try to cheer up Ellie and typed a message on the site saying, *Dear Rosie, can you make a bit of rain cos it's hot here?* They attempted to post the message, but it wouldn't send, so they repeated the same message twice more with no luck. Then they both said very loudly,

"Rosie, hello, HELLO, ARE YOU LISTENING?" All at once a purple flash shot out of the computer, lasting just a couple of seconds. They were both stunned.

"What on earth was that?" Then Scott, Jodie's partner, ran downstairs, looking confused.

"Has there been a power cut? Because the lights in the bathroom have gone off and then came on again. I just saw this flash… in the bathroom!" Ellie, Scott and Jodie all swore that it was absolutely true.

These impromptu evenings, the music and the companionship, saw me through some impossible times. It was only after they had gone home and the house was quiet that I would curl up in the corner by the piano. On those darkest days I wondered if I was going insane but, sharing this with other grief-stricken mothers, realised that we all did it.

I started to attend the local spiritualist church every Thursday evening, finding companionship with other people who simply believed and accepted that our loved ones walk beside us in another dimension, so we cannot see them. This was the most natural thing in the world to them and I became a regular attendee, watching mediums who were able to bring undeniable evidence of survival. I longed for messages from Rosie. David didn't want to accompany me but said he also believed Rosie was around and had himself received messages.

Just after Rosie died, he was driving our car and felt a sharp kick in his back as if it came through the back of his driver's seat. He had always told Rosie off for kicking the seat. He said there was no question he had imagined it. He was convinced she had visited that day to say, "Hey, Daddy, I'm here. I haven't gone anywhere."

Or there was the time when Ellie lost her toy duck. Duck was Ellie's comfort toy which she had loved and needed every night since she was a baby. We looked everywhere. We searched upstairs, downstairs, even out in the garden by torch light in case Alfie had taken it. Then we became fed up because Ellie was making such a fuss. While looking downstairs, I was thinking, come on, Rosie, help us find this duck. David, in the meantime, went into Rosie's room and put his hand on her green papier mâché pig, which they had made together at John Radcliffe.

He said, "Rosie, come on, I can't stand your sister getting in such a bloody state. Now where is this flipping duck?" He came out of the bedroom and went into Ellie's room and a voice said to him "*IN THE FLOWERS!*" On her dressing table was a bouquet of flowers which Ellie had been given at a show the day before and there was the duck in among the stalks.

The Voice in My Head
August 2003

Mum's garden was empty and quiet. Even though the day was hot, I couldn't enjoy the warm summer sunshine and wandered around the garden feeling restless. Normally the girls would have been in Mum's pool or swinging on her old hammock under the dining room window. A friend had taken Ellie out, David had gone to see one of his brothers, and I was alone.

I was standing at the end of the garden, looking down towards the empty hammock, when suddenly I heard Rosie's forthright little voice saying, "Don't talk about it. Do it!" and along with her voice I had the clearest picture in my head, of a baby. It was not that I was trying to imagine it or that I was planning anything myself, but an idea was taking root. Was it really her or was it just me clinging desperately to any passing piece of driftwood in an attempt to stay afloat? Whatever it was there was only one option and that was to try to find a flicker of hope so I could emerge from a very dark tunnel to a place where I could live whatever life I had left without my daughter.

At first, I was so shocked that I couldn't mention it to anybody, particularly David. It felt like betraying our beloved daughter Rosie by even entertaining the thought of having another child. My husband loved his daughters and Rosie's death had broken his heart.

Rosie was not replaceable. With some guilt, I realised that although suffering the worst loss imaginable, somehow I retained the capacity to think of loving another child. While we could never give Ellie back her little sister, a new sibling could be a positive addition, and perhaps in the fullness of time bring her some joy and company. She was now an only child, and it was agonising to watch her learning to be alone. It was the one small, faint flicker of light which I clung to, and which got me through the end of that day, and for the first time that inner voice which I know was Rosie's just kept repeating, "Do it, DO IT."

Rosie's Rainbow Charity Begins
September 2003

It was imperative that Rosie's last wish was carried out, so I called Christine, the senior play specialist at John Radcliffe Hospital. I explained how we wanted to set up some sort of fund to provide a service that would benefit the children Rosie had wished to support. We talked of the conversation Rosie had with Christine on that grey day back in March in the hospital playroom when she had so vehemently expressed her wish. Rosie had watched so many children struggling over the long months when she had been a patient. There must be something we could put in place so that children of all ages, from the babies through to the older teens, could benefit in a holistic and gentle way.

I explained to Christine, "It must be something which represents Rosie's character, and which embraced what Rosie would have liked while she was a patient on the ward." Christine suggested either art or music therapy. I instantly knew that because Rosie's life was filled with music and song, this was the path we should explore. Music therapy would tick all the boxes and encapsulate all we and Rosie had believed in. I began to formulate a plan of action and needed to gather a team together to set the ball rolling.

Through Rosie's illness I was lucky to have the love and support of my trusted group of dear friends. There was never any need to wear my mask for them and I was fortunate to have their loyalty, patience, and understanding day or night.

Helene's own experiences with Ella and the longevity of our relationship meant that we shared common ground. Her husband and David were good mates, and we had a firm lifelong friendship. Her leadership skills were unquestionable, and she had a capacity to get a lot done. Her attention to detail and ability to complete tricky tasks was ideal for the role.

Candice and I had been close friends since our teens as performing arts students. We had spent holidays together and shared a house before she graduated to follow a professional career as a musical theatre performer. She had been a tower of strength with her glass half full attitude and her genuine kindness.

Bev was a dance teacher like me. Reliable, kind, and always supportive, her sound common sense and clear thinking made me feel safe. She was also close friends with Helene.

Gaenor had been there in quiet support since Rosie had been admitted into hospital, offering selfless compassion during those last terrible weeks when she had been on hand to drive me to and from the hospital.

These women all knew Rosie well and it was an easy choice that they became the first Rosie's Rainbow trustees.

So, we all set to work, first drawing up a constitution to become a registered children's charity. Our evening discussions were a huge comfort and support to me. Meetings were filled with planning and hard work for upcoming events, but there was also laughter, meals together, sometimes tears, and always the bond of friendship.

Early in 2004 *Rosie's Rainbow Fund* was registered with the Charity Commission.

We ran a competition amongst Rosie's school friends to design a logo for Rosie's Rainbow Fund. We needed a childlike picture which we could use as our emblem. The kids were enthusiastic and became busy submitting lots of fun designs. The trustees set about judging a winner. The last one on this colourful pile was designed by Emma. She had captured the essence of Rosie perfectly. Her smiling pigtailed 'best friend' was perched on a rainbow in coloured pencil. It had all the details down to the stripy tights. She had drawn two puffy clouds at each end of the rainbow and had written *Rosie's Rainbow Fund* in her childlike font beneath the arch in the same rainbow colours. The fun and colourful design was the unanimous winner and I felt Rosie would have been proud of her friend. Her design was replicated and branded onto our charity letterhead, embroidered on to our staff tee shirts, and used on our charity collection buckets and merchandise.

ROSIE'S RAINBOW FUND

We sourced a music therapist who was working at Helen House Hospice in Oxford. Ceridwen was a passionate but sensitive lady with many years' experience working with terminally ill children. We arranged to meet in Oxford, where I was immediately drawn to her gentle demeanour. She was a highly talented musician and able to play a range of instruments from keyboard to clarinet. Ceridwen was ideal for the post and became our first Rosie's Rainbow music therapist.

Her twice-weekly sessions soon became a lifeline to the children on the wards at John Radcliffe. We purchased a large trolley and filled it with a host of brightly coloured ocean drums, rattles, xylophones, and music therapy instruments. Ceridwen would push the trolley from ward to ward, working her way through the list of children identified by the play team as needing music therapy. She covered all the children's wards, and her music sessions were highly valued and enjoyed by children from small babies to older teens. She was quiet but with a skill to empower the children through the magic of music, allowing them to enjoy a measure of control.

Remembering how Rosie had felt powerless as a patient and how it frightened her that she had no say in anything while she was undergoing treatment, this was an extraordinary, progressive step. The children looked forward to these sessions where they were able to take the lead and to express themselves even if they were unable to talk. They could sing or drum or just listen and relax, and for this period there would be no needles, no painful procedures, just music and colour, encouragement, positivity, and smiles.

Eventually, we implemented group sessions in the covered play area or in the playroom. Children would arrive in their wheelchairs and soon be engrossed, enjoying time with the other children. It touched me to see their parents smiling as they watched their sons and daughters experiencing genuine pleasure and confidence from these sessions. Music therapy was empowering. They had no control over the savage treatment which many of them had to deal with, nor of the pain they were in, but this was a time when the children led the sessions, expertly and cleverly guided by the therapist.

The charity work was gaining momentum of its own and it seemed that no sooner did we hit on a new idea or incentive then the right people would appear to take these ideas forward. I placed my trust in Rosie with the strongest conviction that she was directing each new initiative from her rainbow and that I only had to listen and follow her lead. We gathered a team of fifteen older children from our theatre school and created a programme of songs and a calendar of bookings for our first Rosie's Rainbow Choir tour. Ellie was part of the ensemble. Rosie's Rainbow Choir seemed to be an obvious way to raise awareness and funds through song, and our young performers loved any opportunity to perform, so it was the perfect combination.

We needed a charity anthem, and I could not find one which felt right. I decided to write one instead – or Rosie did! Somehow the words seemed to type themselves onto the page.

I called Machiel. "I have some words here for a new charity song. I think Rosie wrote them."

Sometimes it's hard not to believe
On the other side there is no grief…

The words continued and just flowed and in less than half an hour, I had the whole set of lyrics of the complete song.

In his strong South African accent, he laughed. "No worries. Rosie has been busy. Send them to me." Two days later Machiel called me.

"Come and listen and see what you think."

I printed off my new lyrics, called a rehearsal, and we taught it to the choir. He had composed a beautiful and moving melody for my words. It was perfect.

'You Paint the Rainbow' became the theme song for the charity. The choir went on to sing this anthem at all Rosie's Rainbow shows and events and even on TV and radio. Machiel orchestrated the song, and we recorded it, selling CDs to raise much-needed funds. At every event the song seemed to strike a chord with so many and create an emotional but inspirational finale.

You paint a rainbow of love in the sky
For every human who lives and dies
And it's bringing us strength
And it's bringing us hope
To help your rainbow shine.

We took the choir to John Radcliffe Hospital to sing to the patients, staff, and parents on ward 4B. The singers piled into a minibus. Machiel came too and I was very pleased to have his support that day. Ellie wanted to go, maybe for the same reasons as I did. It felt strange to be making that familiar journey on the M40. The kids were chatting and generally having a good time while I sat on the minibus wondering what the hell I was doing when Machiel said, "Look, Carolyn, it's a rainbow." It stretched from one side of the motorway to the other and we drove straight under it. A few minutes later there was another one. It was as though we were driving under rainbow arches. "You see?" Machiel was chuckling. "Rosie is with us and is not going to be left out of the event."

It was surreal retracing the same path to the ward and leading the choir past the bed where Rosie had been just a few months before. There was another little girl in it. She was oblivious to my stare. Her mum had her back to me, which was probably lucky, and I felt such empathy for that mum and her child. I truly hoped she would have a happier outcome.

Greeted by Christine and several of the nurses I knew well, we went through to the playroom. It was unchanged. There were the familiar tables and the games and some craft equipment in the cupboards, which were still in the same place. Many of the children in our choir were Rosie's school friends and upon arrival I wondered whether bringing them to Rosie's ward was going to overwhelm them. They seemed fine, if taken aback, as they passed some children with no hair and poorly babies in cots on the side wards. Ellie was putting on a very brave face, but I could see she was finding it difficult and trying not to let it affect her.

Arriving in the hospital playroom, the choir arranged themselves and did a vocal warmup, whilst Machiel set up the music system and ran a sound check. A group of young patients trickled in. Some were in wheelchairs or being carried by an adult. Several children were hooked up to drip stands attached to cannulas under bandages on their little hands or attached to ports in their chests.

There were mainly mums with the kids that day. They all looked pale from being trapped indoors and exhausted from worry and sleep deprivation. While the medical care at John Radcliffe was first rate, parents had to deal with intolerable stress. Some were parents of long-term patients who had been in hospital with their children for much longer than I had. Others were there for years with little hope of ever leading a normal life. There was no respite for them. If parents were looked after and nurtured, this would also benefit the children. Parents could be supported to remain emotionally strong and better able to look after their children. Perhaps Rosie's Rainbow could set up a programme to support them too.

The choir sang and the music really lifted the spirits of the onlookers. I was proud of them all. It was emotional, but it was worth it, and the choir sang all the way home on the minibus.

The trustees set about scheduling a calendar of fundraising events. The money to fund music therapy and parent support was steadily growing.

A Rainbow's Light
November 2003

Jenni Thomas invited Ellie and Laura to perform their song, 'A Rainbow's Light', at London's Café Royal at a fundraising ball in aid of her child bereavement charity.

They were honoured to accept and rose to the occasion. Dressed in matching long shimmering dresses, Ellie in soft pink and Laura in a graceful lilac, they gave a moving performance. Since there were many bereaved parents at the ball, their song struck a chord with their audience, and it was very well received.

I contacted a very old friend, Stuart Ongley, who ran a music publishing company and sent him a recording of the songs. Stuart was intrigued to hear the girls' compositions. The next day he called me to say that he had spoken to his friend and work colleague Chris Eaton, who had worked for many years with Sir Cliff Richard. Chris expressed an interest in coming to meet the girls. They came to our house the following week, where the girls sang 'A Rainbow's Light' and 'Does It Rain in Heaven?' for them. Chris was clearly moved by the whole story behind the songs and invited the children to his home, where he would record their song for a CD. Ellie and Laura were hugely excited, and this gave Ellie and me a welcome focus for the next few weeks.

We were on the motorway driving to Chris's recording studio when Ellie gasped. "Mum, look, it's a rainbow!" It was bright and clear, and we drove straight under it before turning off towards Chris's home. I was unsure whether to laugh or cry and so I did both, because I knew that Rosie was not going to be left off this very exciting recording.

Rosie's classmates and their mums asked if they could paint the school lunchroom with a rainbow theme, as a way of coming to terms with their sadness.

They called themselves the Rainbow Brigade and this was their personal tribute to their dear friend. The ceiling and upper walls were painted like sky and clouds and a huge rainbow ran over the ceiling.

On the white paintwork panelling, they copied and stencilled leger lines and the musical notes of Rosie's song 'Enchanted', which she had composed for *Forever and A Day*. There were treble clefs and a melody line in a frieze all around the walls.

To anyone who came to the school unaware of our tragedy, the room just looked pretty and bright. To those who knew, the room felt as though it was filled with Rosie. Large, framed photo collages of all the pantos Rosie had taken part in were hung on the walls. There she was as a mouse in *Cinderella*, a round, cheerful face which grinned from under a brown hood with ears. And there she was in a gingham dress as a village child in *Jack and the Beanstalk*, and a cheeky, small bewhiskered rat in a black wet-look jacket in *Dick Whittington*. With a sudden lurch of my stomach, the realisation hit me that while her friends would probably go on to perform in many more shows, these photos would be the last ones we would ever have of our child.

Her friends were coping with their grief too. I imagined Rosie in the thick of it, helping her mates and generally getting as covered in paint as they were. They wore rainbow headbands, laughed a great deal, and enjoyed being plastered in paint and sucking coloured lollipops. They seemed to have taken on her personality. It was bittersweet – a new word I had to learn to live with.

That week one of the Rainbow Brigade mums called. She had just found a video of Rosie on her kitchen table. She was confused as she hadn't put it there. It had just appeared as nobody else in the house had moved it. The last time she tried to play the video was the previous summer and she was frustrated that it hadn't worked. It was now working perfectly and as soon as she pressed *play*, there was Rosie performing a dance routine at a school assessment. She asked if I would like it and brought it round. I couldn't summon up the courage to watch it but was grateful that I had another memento and amazed that Rosie was still up to her 'pranks'.

As the months went by, David and I were unable to grieve as a couple. A distance grew between us which I tried to ignore but which was undeniable and becoming more difficult to bear. I read somewhere that 99.9% of couples separate after the loss of a child. I clung to the hope that we would make it through and be one of the marriages that survived. However, the gulf between us was widening. He was not able to share his feelings with me. When I was having a particularly bad day, he would be at his most distant. He would disappear to the local gym and unburden his grief to his personal trainer. We silently accepted that we were both so broken that to lean on each other was simply not possible as we couldn't share our pain.

There were many times when I was a mess and he would shout, "For God's sake, don't cry, woman. I can't stand it when you cry." And he would leave the house, and I would hear his van rumble off up the road. He would be gone for hours and each time I would sit and rock or stare at the wall, my stomach in knots.

Much later I found out that on these occasions he would do the forty-minute drive up to John Radcliffe Hospital, where he would park his van and stare up at the fourth-floor window of what had been Rosie's ward. Then he would drive home again, switch on the TV, and stare at that until he would fall asleep on the sofa. He would leave for work next morning before I got up. If either of us were to survive this, then we had to find some way of living with this horror.

The First Birthday Without Rosie
December 2003

Rosie's birthday was looming in December. The Christmas period had always been a season of fun, family, and birthday parties. As the 17th drew closer, I became increasingly worried and frightened about getting through it. Rosie would have been twelve. I was tortured thinking of how she might have marked her birthday had she still been with us.

It felt right to mark the day, but we had no idea how. The day before her birthday, I was in a terrible state. The physical pain in my heart was more intense than it had ever been. I was restless, agitated, wishing to go to sleep and block it out.

My Compassionate Friends shared various ways they would mark the birthdays of their own children. Many would lay flowers on their child's grave, but Rosie had no grave. Some did a balloon release, but that did not feel right either. In the end we didn't plan anything at all. The night before Rosie's twelfth birthday, I kept saying, "Rosie, please just be with me. Please help us all get through it somehow."

Waking up on her birthday, I was aware of a physical heat around my heart. It was as though I was being held tight by something very warm and I felt the strangest sense of peace. Wishing to bottle that sensation and make it last, I believe that some outside force carried me through that day. Ellie and I visited Mum, David saw his brothers, and the day passed. The next day the feeling just wasn't there, but I never forgot that heat. Was Rosie twelve in spirit or was she always going to remain eleven?

There was only a week to go until our first Christmas without Rosie. How would we get through these festive occasions? We needed to try for Ellie's sake. It was impossible for her. The family tried hard to compensate by buying her a lot of presents. It was all they could do. I couldn't face shopping for the cousins, so bought gift vouchers for everyone. It was a very tough time.

The First Show for Rosie
January 2004

We planned a one-night gala concert at the Novello Theatre. Everyone wanted to be part of the show. I asked our very old friend Adam Stafford to act as compère and help with the production. We had known him since he was a small boy with dimples, and he was now a well-respected actor and director.

Rosie had always found him fascinating and watched him perform on many occasions. Following a theatre visit to watch him play Winnie the Pooh when Rosie was six years old, she began calling him Uncle Pooh. The name stuck and she still called him Uncle Pooh when she was eleven. He was only too pleased to be on board with our first gala and we drew up a list of mutual showbiz friends who might be interested in participating. Adam was incredibly generous with his time and talents, and I invited him to become a patron of Rosie's Rainbow. Also joining the list of performers on that night were Mazz and Gina Murray, who, like Adam, were old friends and promised to do all they could to help. They were also more than happy to join the list of charity patrons.

I also added Lucy Benjamin to the roster. As an ex-pupil she had trained at our school from the age of seven and, having achieved success as a child actress, became a household name playing Lisa in *EastEnders*. Lucy made several trips to the hospital to witness our work, watching music therapy sessions, taking time to meet and chat to the patients and parents.

Dr Anne Thomson, Rosie's consultant at John Radcliffe, also accepted the role of patron. It was important to strike a balance and add a medical professional, and she also agreed to come and speak at the concert.

We rehearsed the kids, and a programme began to take shape. David and his brothers also wanted to be a part of the show. None of them had ever been on stage before. They didn't have a clue about theatre and didn't know upstage from downstage, but David had decided that they would perform 'You Can Leave Your Hat On' from *The Full Monty* and so his four brothers, together with a couple of mates, asked Dee to rehearse them for the big night. It was no mean feat choreographing so many large left feet and getting them to count to four at the same time. As the performance drew close, the men became jittery since the routine involved a slow strip, ending in them baring all as the lights went out. Timing was crucial and they were amateurs.

By the day of the dress rehearsal, Dee had managed to make it work and both of us applied a last-minute polish and issued instructions to keep counting, stay calm, and not to down any cans of beer before the performance!

David became something of a self-appointed expert and was heard complaining to his brother Dennis just after the dress rehearsal that he "needed to get the timing right". They left the last rehearsal in high spirits, heading to the tanning salon where they had made a group booking for full body spray tans.

The kids in the show were given strict instructions that they must remain backstage and away from the wings area while the Full Monty was on. Unsurprisingly, they were hatching plans and weren't going to miss Ellie's dad and his brothers' stage debut with orange tans still hidden beneath their navy suits.

The day of the show arrived and the excited kids, West End performers, and David's brothers arrived at the theatre. Adam co-ordinated the show, ready for a brilliant evening. We had a sell-out and the audience arrived, filling the auditorium and buying a lot of raffle tickets. David's friend who worked for British Airways kindly donated four flight tickets to New York. My sister-in-law Tracey ran the bar while her kids George and Annie took on the job of running up and down the stalls handing out beers to the Full Monty 'groupies' who had come along to cheer on the boys. It was an evening where both families united to support Rosie's Fundraiser.

Mum was watching from her usual location at the back of the stalls, and some extra standing room audience squeezed in next to her since it was a full house.

All was going so well that for the first time since Rosie had left us, I felt positive and excited. It was hard to believe that this whole show was because of her but she was not there, although, oddly, I felt she was and wondered if she was sitting in H8, her favourite seat.

The kids were thoroughly enjoying performing and Rosie's Rainbow Choir had sung a couple of medleys. Our West Endies expertly breezed through their numbers and Adam was doing a fabulous job as compère. Then it was time for the Full Monty. The men took their positions. They had the full outfit and we had customised their black trousers so that they were fastened with Velcro and could be whipped off in less than a second, revealing their thongs. It was not a pretty sight, but it was a hilarious one. Their faces were distorted in their effort to remember the moves as they nervously strutted their stuff, items of clothing flying around the stage. As the end of the number drew near, I noticed that Ellie's friends had sneaked into the wings and were crowding round the entrances, cheering and whooping loudly, ready and waiting to watch Ellie's dad, brothers, and mates getting their kit off.

Thankfully the lights went to blackout just on time, saving any embarrassment for the men, but as the red velvet curtains closed, there was a mad scrabbling about when they tried to find their underwear and dressing gowns, since they had been moved by the kids.

The Full Monty
Back Row L-R:
Nigel, Norman,
David.
Front Row L-R:
Dennis, Colin, Tim.

Dr Anne Thomson came onstage and, in her gentle Scottish brogue, spoke about Rosie and her bravery and about how our new charity work was proving so valuable to the children in her care. It felt very odd having her there. My world mixing with the terminally ill world. The applause and laughter of our crowd made me feel uncomfortable, for most of them had no experience of the strains and stresses of life as parents of long-term hospital patients. Of course, it was necessary that they understood that they were fundraising to help these children and parents and they were startlingly generous with their donations that evening.

Then it was time to draw the raffle. Helene had been frantically folding tickets and handed Adam the bucket. Adam swirled his hand around, mixing up the raffle tickets, and called Rosie's best friend Emma to the stage to draw the tickets. Into the red bucket went her hand, swirling the tickets round again. Rosie must have been guiding her little friend's hand. She drew the number and read it out loud.

"It's my ticket." A yell and a collection of loud whoops came from the wings as Ellie was pushed onto the stage. Ellie had won the star prize – the trip to New York New York. We all knew that Rosie had a hand in it – literally. The audience cheered for her. We were in a state of disbelief that out of all the hundreds of tickets sold, Ellie's was the lucky one. We were thrilled and excited too. None of us had ever visited the Big Apple. It was just the treat Ellie needed. That evening we raised £8,000.

What Planet Was I On?
February 2004

It was becoming an obsession to browse through and read as many books as I could from the 'tragic life stories' section at WHSmith which might provide an insight into life on the other side. I had already read three books by the psychic medium Rita Rogers, as well as *Life After Life* by Raymond Moody and *The Wheel of Life* by Elisabeth Kübler-Ross, all of which just confirmed my newfound beliefs. It was a comfort to read *Journey of Souls*, written by Michael Newton, who put many people under hypnosis, and they travelled back in time not just to their past lives but to their spirit world home, which they described as the most wonderful place and their real home to which they all return. I now believed it all and wished I could experience it first-hand. I was desperate to know that Rosie was safe in this parallel plane called the spirit world.

For some reason immersing myself in other peoples' bereavement journeys made me feel less alone. I picked a book from the shelf. It was about murdered schoolgirl Sarah Payne, written by her mother Sara. The last paragraph caught my attention. Sara Payne wrote that following her daughter's death she went on to give birth to another child and that although the new baby could never replace Sarah, it gave her back a tomorrow. Remembering Rosie's voice in my head, I felt that we too deserved a tomorrow.

After tentatively broaching my idea to David, I was relieved that, although sceptical, he agreed that I should make an appointment to see the GP.

The waiting room was full of patients, but I was pretty sure that no one there was about to have the sort of discussion I was going to have. Whoever in their right mind gave birth to a baby at forty-nine? What planet was I on?

Afraid to be pronounced delusional, I was just considering escaping through the fire door when the bell rang, and it was my turn.

Entering through the double doors along the familiar corridor, I knocked on the doctor's door. I spilled out my desire to the GP with a lump in my throat and the growing fear that she would tell me not to be so ridiculous. Amazingly she was understanding and supportive, saying when the time was right, if I still wanted to try for another child, she would back me every inch of the way.

So, a few weeks later I returned for some blood tests to check my ovulation levels.

At forty-nine the results were not promising. However, my GP was still prepared to help and said she would refer me to a fertility expert.

The next hurdle was letting Ellie know. She would either totally flip or would agree it was worth pursuing. Our bereaved teenager had already been through so much turmoil, and this could be a huge stumbling block. But we needed her approval, although I had no idea how to broach the subject.

Ellie was watching TV and there was something on the news about Paul McCartney being a father at sixty years old. Her reaction was extreme.

"It's just disgusting and gross and people shouldn't have babies at that age!"

David and I looked at each other then I looked at Ellie and the whole thing just came out.

"If you go ahead with this, I will leave home and never come back." She was crying. "I will go and live with Grandma. Why are you trying to replace Rosie? I already have a sister and I don't want another one!"

I tried to make her understand.

"Ellie, we haven't got Rosie anymore. There is no way we are replacing her because there could never be another Rosie." She was not ready to listen, but maybe when she had some time to consider, she would come round.

We then decided to tell my sister Sam and Mum. David had misgivings about telling Mum. "We are not asking for her permission. We are presenting this as fact, a fait accompli," I said.

The truth was we didn't know how she would take it. We didn't want to upset her, but I didn't want secrets and needed her to be a part of everything, whatever the outcome.

She was in the kitchen when we arrived. "Mum, we have something to talk to you about. We are not asking your permission, and we know that you will try to talk us out of it, but our minds are made up. We are going to try to have another child."

Her first reaction was of raised eyebrows in disbelief. "I think you are utterly cuckoo," she said. I felt fleetingly angry, but then saw tears in her eyes and could see she was about to cry. "Listen, Mum," I began, then all our rehearsed reasons flooded out.

Always a rational thinker, she said, "You must think how the child will feel when it is fifteen and you are sixty-five years old and taking him or her to school. How do you think the child will feel when all the other mums are so young, and you look like a granny?"

My answer was "Happy that his parents love him so much, I should think." Finally, she accepted the news gracefully.

Mum is a stoic woman, and I am thankful to have inherited her stubbornness and inability to accept defeat. Maybe there were a few of those Jewish genes in me.

Sam was the only one fully supportive. "Go for it. If it's what you truly want, then follow your gut."

Our consultation was arranged with Mr Dimitry at Princess Christian's Hospital in Windsor. Whilst he was sympathetic to our situation, he was less than hopeful that we could conceive naturally.

"I have to be honest with you. There is a one in a thousand chance of conceiving a child naturally. Now, in the unlikely event that it does happen, the risk of miscarrying would be two out of three and the baby would carry a huge and worrying risk of severe foetal abnormalities." He continued, "It is possible to give you treatment to boost your ovulation, but there is a risk of developing ovarian cancer."

My heart sank. The statistics and the cancer risk came as a shock.

"What about adoption?" he asked.

He suggested we go abroad and give an unwanted child a life. We should forget having our own child by natural means.

That is, unless we chose IVF with a donor egg.

Our chances of success would then jump to 50%. This, though, would mean that although it would be David's genetic child, it wouldn't be mine. It would have someone else's genetic blueprint. Sometimes it was possible to use an egg from a family donor. This would enable family genes to continue, but in his experience, it could cause issues within the family, subjecting the new child to interference from the family egg donor. There was the potential for causing serious family problems with the blurred lines of this sort of relationship.

The homeward journey back to Maidenhead was silent except for David emphatically saying he was "absolutely not up for adoption".

My hopes for a future with prams, nappies, a houseful of kids, and playdates were dented.

Sam called me to hear the doctor's verdict. I had not mentioned Mr Dimitry's suggestion of using a family egg donor. I was startled, therefore, when she immediately and unprompted said, "You can use my eggs. I am offering my own eggs!"

I asked her to think very seriously before committing herself to such a huge undertaking. She remained adamant. "Caro, the child would then carry our family genes, so it would be the same as using your own egg. It would be an egg I won't be using for anything else."

I broke the news to David, who reluctantly agreed to pursue this new idea and Sam's offer. So, we would be on the case after the weekend.

Meanwhile Ellie was already struggling with the plan, and it was even worse when she found out that her aunty Sam was offering to be the egg donor.

She broke down.

"That's disgusting. The baby wouldn't be my brother or sister. It would be a cousin."

She stormed up to her bedroom and slammed the door.

I wrote a letter to her explaining everything again and begging her to reconsider. I slid the letter under her bedroom door. She wouldn't listen to me anymore.

I felt sorry for us both and hated myself for what I was doing to my daughter when she was already in such pain. Two days later she appeared to have calmed down a little and we drove to Windsor. We did some clothes shopping and I tried to spoil her and bought her a selection of new tops and girly stuff before going for lunch at Daniel Department Store. As we walked through the baby department, Ellie lifted a little pink baby designer outfit off the rail.

"Isn't that lovely?" she said. I smiled with huge relief.

Then she snapped, "No, not for YOUR baby, for MINE when I have one." It was a punch in my gut. We managed lunch, but I felt winded and sick all afternoon. We drove home in silence, and she didn't talk to me until bedtime.

I told Mum how badly Ellie had taken it, but she said it wasn't surprising.

"Ellie said it would be like having a cousin, not a brother or sister."

"Well, it will rather, won't it?" said Mum. I flew at her in anger and told her never ever to say that again.

So, we had a very angry daughter, a mum who had no option but to deal with it, and my sister who was up for doing whatever it took to make this work. She had spoken to Phil, who was willing to be as helpful as he could.

David was reluctant to proceed after the traumatic episode with Ellie, but we both hoped she would at some point come round to the idea.

Eloise at the New York Plaza
April 2004

Ellie's winning raffle ticket meant that we had something positive and exciting to look forward to. Thanks to the friend from British Airways who organised our flights, we travelled first class from Heathrow. Ellie invited Laura as her travel companion, while I asked Jayne since David didn't want to go. She always kept in touch and lately we had spent a lot of time together. She had been there for me over the past few months and one of those people who did not shy away from talking about my grief.

Ellie was asked to choose the hotel, so she picked the Plaza overlooking Central Park. She chose it since she had read the book *Eloise at the Plaza* as a small girl and Eloise was her real name. It was a very grand hotel with much ostentatious gold and gilt. Laura shared a huge bedroom with Ellie while I shared with Jayne.

We window shopped on Fifth Avenue and booked some awesome Broadway shows.

At the very top of the Empire State Building, I looked down at the tiny dots of humanity and yellow taxis below and wondered how on earth it was that my child was chosen to be the unlucky one. Why was it not that dot down there, or that one?

As my eyes skimmed the New York skyline, the Chrysler Building, Central Park, Times Square, Ground Zero, I thought how small and insignificant my grief appeared from this viewpoint above the world.

We took our seats in the auditorium, awaiting curtain up on *Forbidden Broadway*. I was so looking forward to the popular off-Broadway show, but the next moment I was sobbing, seated in the centre of the row with no tissues, trying not to draw attention to myself. Seconds later the show began, and I wondered how in the hell I could be weeping for my dead child one minute and then laughing at the spoof to the tune from *Annie* the next.

Our hotel bedroom at the Plaza overlooked Central Park. It

was grand and ornate with gilt furnishings echoing the style of the illustrations in *Eloise at the Plaza*. Jayne, in her sweet and caring way, just sat on the bed, her arm around me. I was blubbing like a baby, so she found a box of tissues in the bathroom. There were soon damp balls of tissue all over the oversized bed. Catching sight of my reflection in the hotel mirror, my face was unrecognisable with a red nose, blotchy face, and smeared mascara.

During that evening Jayne said that should Sam not be able to produce eggs, she would offer hers. I was so touched by this gesture and her kindness made it possible to get through another evening.

That same evening in their own hotel room, Ellie and Laura were holding long conversations about the whole business. Ellie confided in her fifteen-year-old buddy about the possibility of the new baby. I do not know what Laura said to Ellie that evening, but whatever it was, it changed things.

Back in London, jet-lagged and miserable, I was about to go to the bank to exchange some dollars when Ellie suddenly said, "Mum, are you still thinking of having this baby?"

I took a deep breath. "Yes, we are really hoping to, Els, but you know it may not necessarily happen."

"I have been thinking about it very hard for a very long time and I have decided that while it's not what I would choose for myself, I can understand your reasons. It's cool, Mum, and I'm behind you. You have my total support. I talked to Laura a lot while we were in New York. She thinks it's a great idea too."

"I can't believe you're saying all this, Ellie."

I felt the tears pricking my eyes and my voice shaking. I told her what a huge relief it was to hear her say this after feeling unable to discuss it with her for so long.

"I want to share in choosing the name and buying all the baby stuff and everything," she said.

She also described a very real dream she had about Rosie while she was in New York. Rosie had come to her, and they had been discussing what Rosie can see from where she is. Ellie had asked her whether she is watched while she is in the toilet, but she was told no, but "I see Mummy has a baby in her tummy, and it's a boy." Ellie described Rosie as looking happy and just as she had always been. Then she told me I should be happy that she was now feeling like this and to please stop crying. I hugged her very tight and just wanted to shout to everyone in the High Street, "Listen, everyone, I have my daughter back."

She laughed at me and just said in her best American accent, "Have a nice day!" In my head I thanked Rosie for her help.

The Lister Hospital
May – July 2004

The clock was ticking. I was now nearly forty-nine and Sam was almost thirty-nine. Sam's age was a concern because even thirty-eight was pushing it as egg donors are usually considerably younger.

I left a message with Mr Dimitry again, explaining that my sister had offered to be our egg donor. He telephoned to say that it was a possibility and that he was referring us to the Lister Hospital in Chelsea. I asked him if it could really work for us. His answer was "Absolutely."

I was pleased that at least it was a positive answer.

I sent an email to Sir Robert Winston at his IVF clinic in Hammersmith Hospital to check the facts regarding our ages. A reply arrived later that day, stating that yes, it was all possible, although the guideline age set by the Human Fertilisation and Embryology Authority (HFEA) for egg donors was maximum thirty-seven years of age but that we could appeal to have it lifted. Both he and Mr Dimitry advised we must all undergo counselling before we were permitted to go forward.

Sam, David, Phil, and I made a counselling appointment at the Lister Hospital. The counsellor told us to expect a rollercoaster ride. Frankly, every day since Rosie had left us had been a rollercoaster, so this was not news to me. She suggested some holistic treatments, perhaps some massage to put us in a calm state.

Phil asked a lot of questions, expressing some concern for Sam's health, and wanted to know all the ins and outs. While all this was understandable, Sam, David, and I just wanted to get on with it. With his questions answered Phil left with David and both headed back to work while Sam and I waited for the doctor.

The counsellor said she had marked our file with a special sticker which would show anyone else handling our treatment that we had experienced 'a sadness'. She seemed unable to say the word death. Sam and I were ushered in to see the doctor. He drew some very complicated diagrams, explaining how the process worked, and we left the hospital with two large bags full of drugs. My bag contained contraceptive tablets, pessaries, and Synarel to sniff, which would reduce my oestrogen in preparation for the upcoming treatment. Sam's bag contained drugs to boost her egg production.

On our return, I stopped at Dee's house and found her making tea for the girls. Ellie was inside with Laura. I could hear them playing the piano.

On Dee's front doorstep I filled her in on the day's events and confided we were going ahead. "Look over there," said Dee, pointing upwards. The sky was that sort of dark vivid violet-grey you get when there is... And there it was! A double rainbow against the dark grey sky.

"There you go." Dee laughed. "She approves. Rosie says it's okay."

Ellie came running out of the house and immediately took a photo of the rainbow on her mobile. David phoned me from work. "Do you see what I see?"

"I can see it alright," I told him. "It's the most amazing rainbow I have ever seen."

The next month passed in a flurry of end of term activity. Reports had to be written, days of ballet, tap, and modern dance exams to organise with coaching and exam days to arrange.

At the beginning of July, we held our annual performance assessments in the Novello Theatre, where all our pupils were assessed in every genre – singing, dancing, and acting. Rosie used to enjoy this opportunity to perform. This year felt hard, seeing some of her classmates progressing through their first school year without her, but I had the upcoming treatment to think about, so that helped. The doctor at the Lister had given me a three-week course of contraceptive pills which I had already started taking.

I had been taking the contraceptive pill for three weeks and put on a lot of weight, so was relieved to discard the rest of the packet as directed and move to the next stage. I was quite nervous; this was suddenly real. But we had to be in it to win it.

I started the Synarel treatment. One squirt sniffed into each nostril twice daily. It seemed a very simple thing to do to achieve a living miracle.

The IVF Stage
August 2004

Sam and I were ready to move on to the next stage of the treatment. The last week had been frustrating. Sam's cycle didn't kick in when it should have done, and we had to cancel the previous week's scan and wait. I was beginning to see why they described this as a rollercoaster. With grief to contend with as well, we were having a bumpy ride. August 20th was the date set for egg retrieval.

Now that it was all a reality, I was nervous, excited, and terrified in case it didn't work. I had set such store by the success of this venture. It was the one thing that prevented me from sinking into the abyss. How would I deal with failure? However, nothing could be worse than what we had already lived through.

On August 8th we arrived at the Lister in the pouring rain. I was handed a course of tablets while Sam was given instructions on how to inject herself with Clomid for the next nine days, starting on August 9th. This magic potion was packed in a smart blue case that I imagined Rowan and Sasha would be fighting over to use as a lunch box. The injections would stimulate egg production and if she became bloated, it would be a good sign that she was producing lots of eggs. While I did not want her to experience any discomfort, at the same time I hoped she would be telling me in a few days that none of her trousers fitted!

Lena, our Irish nurse, informed us that they would take about six eggs, fertilise them, and implant two. The remaining embryos would be frozen for the time being and could be stored for up to five years. This extraordinary technology meant that it could be possible to try again if the treatment failed or could maybe become a sibling in the future.

Alternatively, we could donate the embryos to another recipient, give them back to Sam, donate them to research, or they could perish on their own. The chance of success halves with freezing, but Lena pointed out that many pictures of new-born babies on the wall of the corridor were success stories resulting from frozen embryos.

I was constantly amazed by the calmness of the whole setup at the assisted conception unit. But I suppose it was all routine to them.

The waiting room was always full of couples with their own sad stories to tell. They arrived from all over the world, including the Middle East and Africa. They were all wrapped up in their own thoughts, oblivious to anybody else, unlike Sam and me, who could not help people watching. This was probably a throwback to character study in our drama training, and Sam mentioned that she thought there were a lot of incredible TV dramas sitting all around us.

The notice board in the assisted conception department carried leaflets about twin clubs, counselling for desperate wannabe parents, adverts for extremely expensive private hospitals for those lucky enough to have conceived, and a large notice informing women awaiting egg transfer not to empty their bladders on arrival. Since it was usual to be kept waiting for extended periods, I was worried that I would be sitting there a few days later desperately in need of the loo and hoped that on our big day they would keep to the appointment time.

As the days passed, the hormones prescribed were making me tetchy and short-tempered. The slightest thing seemed to trigger tears. By mid-August I was a miserable mess.

Ellie pointed out that I could be pregnant in two weeks' time. The week had dragged, and I wished there was something I could do to speed up the process. As a family we were not the type to sit back and wait and I was not good at hanging about. We had always been 'let's do it' sort of people. This could not be rushed though.

Sam's ultrasound scan revealed three large and two small egg follicles. Maybe we needed to prepare for twins!

My scan fell on Monday, August 16th, Ellie's sixteenth birthday. I was informed that my uterus was perfect, having reached a thickness of ten. The nurse had pointed out three thin lines on the monitor. These were carefully measured and indicated the state and thickness of the uterine lining. They hoped that egg recipients achieved a level of 7.5, and my uterus exceeded that, so they were all smiles.

It was now a question of Sam's eggs reaching an acceptable size. It would just be a few more days then the eggs should be ready.

She had to be on standby to go into the Lister for her egg harvest and David would be required to 'do his stuff'. All I could do was remain detached and calm. Ellie seemed excited and quite positive. She had been shopping in Bicester Village with Shirley, Rosie's nurse from John Radcliffe. I was glad we had struck up a friendship with Shirley. Ellie bonded with her after she had looked after Rosie for so long and they now had a special relationship. She joked that she had a way of getting people pregnant. It made me laugh when she told me she did a sort of fertility dance. I instructed her to keep prancing round her garden.

Twenty-four hours later, Wednesday 18th, Sam rang from the Lister. They had four egg follicles which they could use, and they were going to harvest them on Friday, August 20th. They informed Sam that in younger women they could collect as many as twenty-one eggs but reassured her that although there were only four, this should not be a problem and they all looked like good ones.

Timings were crucial. Sam had to be at the Lister on Friday the 20th by 7am. David had to give his sperm sample at 9:30am, but precisely at that time I would be leaving for Paris with Ellie and her seven friends for her birthday treat! We had planned something special for Ellie's birthday. The trip was not transferrable, and anyway, she was entitled to a treat despite our crazy plans. Bad timing? Yes, possibly, and it was not quite what I had in mind, but I had to leave everything to Sam and David for the time being. My last sniff was that evening before starting the Cyclogest the next morning. It really was happening. I would be in for egg transfer after the weekend.

I bought Sam a token gift – a rainbow candle, a book about sisters, and a card with a cherub sitting on a rainbow. I had no idea what I could give her that would be repayment enough for what she was doing for me. She remained calm and pragmatic about the procedure. When she told me that the two big injections which they gave her at seven and eight o'clock yesterday evening had the ability to cause OHSS, which is ovarian hyper stimulation syndrome, I recalled how bloated she had looked at Sasha's birthday tea the day before. She was very brave. Whatever the outcome it was an act of total generosity which I will never forget. Phil was doing his part too. He had kept his diary free all week to be on hand to look after Rowan and Sasha when the time came. He appeared philosophical and willing to go along with it all.

David seemed okay about everything and arranged to take Sam up to the hospital in the morning.

On Thursday I drove over to Sam's house with my totally inadequate gifts. I had the rainbow cherub to try to say thank you, although words felt insufficient for something of this magnitude. I tried to write that even if the outcome was not what we hoped for, I would never forget this act of generosity. There were butterflies in my stomach just thinking about the coming weekend.

Driving back to Maidenhead, there was another rainbow. It lasted all the way from Wheeler End to home. I had a hunch there would be one that day, like the rainbow after the rain, the hope after the despair. This had to be Rosie's message.

On the telephone Sam sounded reassured and heartened by the rainbow. In my head I thanked Rosie. I tossed and turned all night and then woke at three o' clock in the morning.

At 5.45am on Friday, August 20th, Sam arrived at our house, ready to leave with David for London. She looked as though she hadn't slept either and was nervous about the day's procedure.

David suddenly exclaimed he had forgotten something and disappeared out to his van. He returned with a copy of *Mayfair*. That broke the tension and caused some mild hysteria because we pointed out that he couldn't really walk into the Lister Hospital carrying that. I suggested he put it in a carrier bag, but he discarded it and said he would read theirs! Sam thought they probably had better ones anyway.

I waved them both off. Looking down at my hands, I realised they were trembling. Then with Jayne, Ellie, and seven of her school friends, we all left for Paris.

All the way to Waterloo on the minibus, Ellie and her friends created a noisy and excited hubbub. I couldn't believe that here I was on my way to gay Paree while David and my sister were going about the business of making us a baby!

At the exact moment we arrived at the Eurostar terminal, Sam was under general anaesthetic, having her eggs harvested. Whilst we ate Danish pastries at Waterloo waiting for our train, David was being ushered along the corridor at the Lister, instructed to perform, and then ring the bell when he had finished. Apparently, he dumped the magazines and ran like the clappers, but not before giving a knowing and sympathetic look to the chap in the opposite cubicle whom he supposed must be there for the same reason!

He spent the morning waiting for Sam, wandering around Sloane Square window shopping and looking at the delicatessens but unable to buy anything as he had given me all the money for the Paris trip.

On arrival in Paris, we herded our excited group of kids onto the metro.

Arriving at the hotel, I telephoned home to see if David was back. He had just returned and assured me that the whole procedure had gone to plan, and that Sam was recovering on the hammock in the garden and there was nothing to worry about.

When I finally spoke to her later that day, her drowsiness had worn off and she was feeling fine and happy about everything.

They managed to harvest four eggs, which were taken off to be fertilised in their test tubes – their 'hotel' for the next three days.

Meanwhile Jayne and I spent the remainder of this rather surreal day trooping around the centre of Paris with Ellie and her teenage school buddies, momentarily distracted by two of the boys pratting about performing ballet plies in the middle of the Champs-Élysées. French taxis whizzed past, almost giving me a heart attack, and the same lads climbed over a wall by the Eiffel Tower and tried to look as though they were in a drama by falling into the Seine. If I hadn't been so fond of them, they would have been sent back to the hotel in disgrace.

That night we cruised down the River Seine. The kids loved it and were entranced by the illuminated Eiffel Tower and all the other floodlit buildings.

I wished that Rosie was with us to enjoy the magic of the riverboat cruise. On the way back to the hotel, I picked up a white feather, showed it to Jayne, and popped it into my handbag. We were all footsore and exhausted and fell into our comfortable beds and slept like babies. Before falling asleep, Jayne said she wished we could understand more about the afterlife, or spirit world, or wherever it was that Rosie was directing this excursion from.

Continental breakfast in the hotel dining room had to be delayed on Saturday morning due to eight exhausted kids who couldn't get out of their beds. I was awake at 6.30, my mind racing, but by the time I had roused Jayne and waited for the kids to appear, it was already 9.30.

We joined the two-hour queue outside the Eiffel Tower. An hour and nine ice creams later, I switched on my mobile and there was the message for me to call the hospital.

Distancing myself from the throng, and leaving Jayne to supervise, I dialled England underneath the Eiffel Tower.

"Morning, Carolyn, we have some news for you. Three eggs of the four have fertilised, which is great, and we would like you to come in for the egg transfer on Tuesday the 24th at 10.30. Drink two glasses of water at 10am. We will implant two eggs."

I don't suppose that anyone had ever stood under the Eiffel Tower on that spot and had that conversation!

How surreal that while I was sightseeing in Paris, my future child, with all his or her physical attributes and genetic blueprint already determined, could be waiting for me.

Clicking off the mobile, I imparted the news to Jayne. Ellie was looking at me questioningly across the queue, so I called her over and quietly told her the news. She smiled and gave me a squeeze, then rushed back to her friends and whispered to Laura.

Talented Eggs
Monday, August 23rd, 2004

Back in Maidenhead after the lovely three-night Paris trip, I dumped the cases and went straight to Redroofs school office where Sam was looking surprisingly well. She wished me luck for the transfer the next day, casually dropping into the conversation that she didn't think she would want to go through the procedure again. It had been a physically challenging time, and she was relieved that her part was now over.

Mum was also in the office, inquisitively asking a lot of questions. I tried my best to explain that no, they don't put the egg in first and inseminate afterwards. That was what the test tube was for! She laughed at my graphic description of David doing the deed and told me to avoid the bumps on the way back in case it fell out. I spent the rest of the day chilling as much as I could between supermarket shopping, clearing up, and walking the dog. My nerves were getting the better of me and I couldn't sit still for long.

Tuesday, August 24th

Waking at 5am, I felt apprehensive and restless. David agreed to accompany me to the hospital, although I knew he was forcing himself. Previously he said that he did not want to be in the room when they implanted the embryos. Although I was upset about this, I decided not to make this this an issue or put him under pressure. I understood his worry and the memory of the scan machine and medical equipment might be too painful a reminder. He seemed okay, but then I noticed him staring at the photos of Rosie on the dining room wall and he looked so sad.

We both had to deal with this guilt. It was pointless feeling guilt and disloyalty to Rosie, but it was still there. There was no going back now. Once the eggs were out of their test tube and inside me, the outcome of this life-changing decision would be in the lap of the gods.

I begged Rosie to let me know it was alright, but that day I couldn't hear her answer. Despite being the driving force behind this mission, I felt like a crazy woman and deep down still a grieving mummy.

As we parked the car and arrived at the entrance to the Lister, David had relaxed a little. My bladder was full. I was very fidgety and needed the toilet.

Suddenly David said, "Listen, if you are going to change your mind, now is the time."

"For God's sake, of course I'm not changing my mind. Just shut up and stop going on at me." I was almost crying.

The receptionist asked breezily, "What are you here for today, my love?"

"Embryo transfer." I could hear the tremor in my voice.

"No problem," she said as if our appointment bore no more importance than arriving at the dentist for a routine scale and polish. "Have a seat, my love. The doctor will be along in a moment." I crossed my legs as well as my fingers and prayed it wouldn't be too long.

Thankfully it was not, and a charming Dr Tham showed me into one of the treatment rooms. It was clean, white, and clinical. He explained that the hospital was conducting trials on all egg recipients to examine the success of IVF in tandem with the immune system and could he take some blood?

Yes, yes, I thought, but just hurry up, as I was so uncomfortable.

"I am delighted to tell you that all three embryos have a cell count of eight. That means they are superior. We have one grade A and two grade B. There is hardly anything to choose between them all. They are all first class."

I was smug. It was the stage mother in me. We had talented eggs!

It wasn't long before a very jolly nurse explained that they would implant two embryos and not to worry as it was a painless procedure, no more uncomfortable than a smear test. I was anxious to ask the million-dollar question.

"Can you tell me how you choose which two embryos to implant and which one to leave behind?"

"We leave that to the experts in the lab. Now get ready and Dr Tham will be with you shortly."

A framed poem on the wall written by two grateful parents after the successful birth of their IVF baby kept me distracted for a couple of minutes until he was ready.

"Hello again. Right, we have everything in place, and in a moment, you will see your embryos."

A hatch in the wall swung open on the right of my bed and a nurse popped her head out. It was rather like the drive-thru at McDonald's. "Hi," she said brightly.

Through the hatch, she checked my name and date of birth. "Guess what I have for you?" she chirped. I almost expected her to say Big Mac meal with extra-large fries and a coke. "Your embryos. Here we are." A test tube filled with pink water appeared through the hatch.

"Right, let's do it." My doctor smiled, and before I knew it, my legs were in the stirrups, and the transfer began. I stared at the two monitors.

To the right of one screen appeared two circles. "Those," said the nurse, "are the embryos. You see how many cells they have?" It was certainly a moment I'd never forget. I compared them to the embryos on the wall poster. They looked pretty similar. "Now you will see the syringe as it collects your embryos." My eyes were glued. "Now," said the nurse, "if you watch the other screen…"

She was pressing hard on my bladder with the scanning device. Trying not to think about the discomfort, I attempted to savour that moment as they were introduced into what I prayed would be a nine-month rented but well-furnished accommodation! Although my living quarters were a little antique and possibly in need of some refurbishment, I hoped beyond all hope that they liked it enough to sign the tenants' agreement and stay put – rent free!

And then the job was done. There were smiles all round and instructions to keep taking all the medication.

I was given a large pack of syringes with Gestone to use as backup, only in case of emergency. This would help to prevent shedding of the womb lining. I was told to call the hospital if necessary and they would show me how to use it. "Goodbye," said the jolly nurse. "Pregnancy test in two weeks."

David and I left the hospital, crossing Battersea Bridge towards the car park, carrying the pack of syringes, three weeks supply of Progynova, a packet of crisps, and a ham sandwich. David was more relaxed. "Well, we have done all we can now. They have had Sam's *follicles*, my *bollicles*, and your *trollicles*, so that's it."

That joke broke the tension and made us laugh.

I got straight on the phone to Sam, then Mum, then followed up text messages from various friends saying how much they hoped for good news.

When we arrived home, Ellie gave me a bunch of mini yellow roses and a big hug, which meant more than anything. I slept for an hour that afternoon, during which time she arranged the roses in the glass jug, polished the coffee table, and even tidied the kitchen. This was unusual, and I was so touched. Mum popped over with a pot plant and a card which said, *Good luck and may your eggs be poached to perfection. With love from Grandmother Hen.*

The next day I had a crashing headache. It was probably a reaction to the stress and excitement of the day before. I decided to put up with it, not wanting to take any drugs which could harm my embryos. The day was passing slowly.

Ellie and I spent the next evening with a group of friends from our old antenatal meetings. We had become friends sixteen years earlier, five pregnant ladies with high hopes and dreams for our children, who used to have nothing better to talk about than whether the cabbages they placed on their breasts between feeding the babies made any difference to the soreness. We spent many idle coffee mornings comparing notes in those good old days when we bonded over feeding, teething, weaning, nappies, and comparing nurseries. We were an invincible band of yummy mummies proud of our babies as they fed, crawled then toddled, gained siblings, went to school, grew up, and became teenagers. Ellie and the children were now sixteen and they chatted about their recent GCSE results. Ellie had made us so proud when she had received her GCSE results the previous week. Despite everything, even in her immense grief, she achieved good grades in seven subjects.

I reflected on what a different life most of us were living to that which we envisaged when we proudly cooed and fussed over our new babies. Between us we had notched up three broken marriages. Several of the group had dealt with divorce and sadly one had faced the death of her husband. None of the others had experienced child loss though. Over coffee and cake, I brought them up to date with the news that I had just had two embryos implanted. There was a stunned silence, and their mouths literally fell open. They found it hard to comprehend, but they seemed excited and happy that here was something positive in my life.

There followed a few days of highs and lows. One minute happiness and the next minute tears. I spent a great deal of time on the internet trying to find pictures of five-day-old embryos without much success. It was probably too early, but I needed to get to know them already. I swung between positivity and fear the test would show negative.

On Bank Holiday Sunday we met for a family meal at TGI Friday's in High Wycombe. Sam, Phil, and I took Ellie, Rowan, Sasha, and Molly-May, who was down from Harrogate to stay with her father Robin. My brother Robin and Helen were now divorced. Helen and the kids had moved to Harrogate whilst Robin took a flat in London. We discussed the week's events with Robin while the little ones coloured their table mats and ate pasta. I noticed Molly-May was drawing rainbows. I wondered how well she remembered Rosie. Perhaps being so young, she would have already forgotten. At the end of the meal, Molly-May tore off a piece of paper and wrote *ROSSIE* on it in her neatest six-year-old handwriting and stuck it to her red balloon. She was joined by Rowan and Sasha, who also wrote *Rosie* with crayon on scraps of paper, licking them to make them stick on. Ellie took the three little ones outside and watched the balloons sail up to Rosie in the sky. In the old days, Rosie and Ellie often did that. I cried all the way home, wondering if my embryos would be affected by my sadness.

If only there was some sort of indication that I might be pregnant, the wait would be more bearable. I had been whispering to my embryos all day and trying to stay positive but kept thinking that they may not even be there by now. How would I cope if they were not? I had put so much store by the success of this transfer. The phrase 'Putting all my eggs in one basket' summed it up. I still had to get through another seven days. All I kept thinking was bring on the morning sickness because at least it would be a sign!

We had one of our Bank Holiday family days at Redroofs, which were becoming increasingly difficult to bear.

My three youngest nieces vanished up to the school costume department upstairs. They made an entrance in forty-year-old old-fashioned pale blue nylon leotards which they had unearthed from the bottom of a box. They were baggy round their bottoms from being washed too many times and the blue was faded. They insisted we watch a rather strange performance of *Felicity Wishes meets Angelina Ballerina* in the little forty-two-seater theatre at the back of Mum's house. This was followed by the same cast of uninhibited five- and six-year-olds presenting act two, which consisted of a raunchy rendition of the *Full Monty* musical and then 'Cell Block Tango' from *Chicago*. *These might be my embryo's cousins*, I thought.

In the other room Ellie and her cousins Emily and L-J were at the old baby grand, the three of them squashed together on one stool, composing a new song. I could hear them in full voice, singing their latest composition written that afternoon, "*When you went to sit on the rainbow…*" The girls were all in harmony, singing about their missing cousin Rosie.

Pregnancy Test
September 2004

There was just one week to go till the pregnancy test. For seven days since the transfer, I had been plagued with a sore throat, cough, and bad chest, but was not prepared to take any medication that could affect the embryos.

Fretting and worried, I turned to my friend Val. She had been a professional actress then producer and teacher, and we had known each other for a long time. Val and her partner Ollie were seasoned experts on IVF and succeeded in having three sons. Val and I shared many heartfelt conversations as well as a mutual love for all things spiritual. She was reassuring and reminded me that most people have at least three attempts.

Ellie and I went to admire Rowan and Sasha's four new fish and a rabbit they had christened Fudge Broccoli Rainbow. Sam sensed my highly sensitive mood and immediately knew why. With only five more sleeps until the pregnancy test, I was now coughing like a trooper.

Sam and I met Lucy Benjamin for an al fresco lunch overlooking the river at Maidenhead Bridge. She seemed unaware of *EastEnders* fans staring at her in awe across the tables and the waitress wildly miming *look who's here* to her friend as I filled her in on the treatment. Lucy, one of our old and dearest pupils and almost family, was so intrigued. "That is enormous! No wonder you didn't tell me on the phone."

"Maybe I should freeze my eggs too," she said thoughtfully. "Then I can use them at any time. How long can they stay in the freezer?" I related the whole saga, interspersed with a lot of coughing. Lucy insisted we should please let her know on Tuesday.

Calling into the chemist to pick up a prescription for David, I also asked for cough mixture and questioned the pharmacist about the safety of it in pregnancy as if I was buying it for a friend. "How far gone is the pregnancy?" asked the lady in the white coat.

"Oh, I'm not sure how far gone my friend is!" They suggested glycerine, lemon, and honey, which I purchased for my 'friend', and I left the chemist stifling a cough.

For several days David appeared to have detached himself from the idea and more worryingly detached himself from me. It was probably just his coping mechanism.

On Sunday, September 5th, counting down with just two more days to get through, I finally bought a predictor test, burying it under a bottle of shampoo and conditioner in my shopping basket. The packet read *Unmistakeable results, clear results for the greatest certainty. Over 99% accurate. No more blue lines, just Pregnant or Not Pregnant.* Reading through the instructions in the car and realising I needed to practise, I wished I hadn't told so many people, but on the other hand, it was good to know they were counting down alongside me. There would be a lot of telephone calls to make if the news was negative.

Locking myself in the toilet, I leaned on the door, trying to steady my breath and shaking hands, which were cold and sweaty. This was it. My heart was thumping. After months of planning and hoping, the lines on the test would either mark the beginning of a new chapter or the brutal end of the dream. Oh God, I thought, just feel the fear and do it anyway. A few minutes later confirmation appeared on the stick.

Not Pregnant.

I stared at the *Not Pregnant* on the display and thought it can't be, but it was. I had let David and Ellie down, and expected so much from my sister, having really put her through it. The worst thing of all was the realisation that all the signs and messages from Rosie from the day she left us – which had given me hope that she was still close – must have been my imagination. I felt Rosie was so far away, further away than she had ever been.

I went into the kitchen to break the news to David. Alfie trotted happily around my feet as I held the predictor. I wished I could be as carefree, having really tried to prepare myself for that moment. All the months of prenatal vitamins, folic acid, and hope just seemed to dissolve in that split second of looking at the *NOT* word. And in those few minutes, Rosie seemed to vanish too. And I felt bereft all over again, because all the rainbows, butterflies, and feathers faded to nothing and the 'knowing' she was guiding me turned into a black void.

David said, "Well, if it isn't, it isn't, and we will have to try again, won't we? After all, you paid to have Sam's last egg kept in the freezer."

"No!" whispered Sam on the phone. "No, no, I can't believe it. I was so sure," she said repeatedly. It was a brief call and she said she would phone back.

Mum was also disappointed. I needed to hear her sound reassuring. She had always been the voice of reason and good sense in the past. She had been unable to offer that since the death of Rosie. The phone was ringing, my mobile bleeping, and I imparted the bleak news to other family members and friends. What an idiot I was to have told so many people about our IVF treatment. Why on earth did I share it with so many when it would have saved the embarrassment and pain of telling them we had failed?

David escaped to work, while I took the dog out, hoping that a trip to my usual dog walk field might help me get a grip and decide on a course of action. When I returned, Ellie was up and appeared in the living room doorway. I couldn't get the words out, so just shook my head. She looked crestfallen. "Well, you'll just have to do it again, won't you?" It was interesting that both my husband and daughter had some words of encouragement.

I owed it to my disappointed daughter to try and get through the day together. She needed me to be with her and thank God I had her.

Before we left the house, I phoned the IVF unit at the Lister and spoke to one of the nurses. She said she was very sorry but then suggested I go on testing for a few days as sometimes it takes longer for the HCG to trickle in. Startled to be given this glimmer of hope, I passed the news around.

Ellie dragged me off to Slough and whisked me around lots of shops. We arrived home with twenty-eight pairs of satin pyjamas for our upcoming Aladdin pantomime and twenty red and white polka dot skirts at a knock-down price from Primark, which I would use for the next Rosie's Rainbow Fund show. The trip provided a distraction and gave me a focus for the day.

David was very quiet when he arrived home that evening. Joining him in the living room, we stared at the television, sipping our coffee in silence.

Despite the home kits being fairly accurate, the Lister Hospital asked me to go for a blood test to confirm the result. After the hospital blood test, they would phone in a few days with a definite yes or no. I enquired whether they could unfreeze the remaining embryo and just pop it in, but the response was that I would have to start the treatment cycle again. Having been pumped with too much progesterone, all my hormone levels would be out of sync.

As expected, when they called from the Lister Hospital, I was not pregnant. On hearing this I remained strangely calm, telling myself not to be so easily defeated.

I wondered at what point the embryos had decided not to stay. Was it due to external factors and feeling so unwell or were they just not strong enough to survive? There was no way of knowing. I went to the doctor, who immediately prescribed an antibiotic for the chest infection, which had really laid me low.

We had one more egg cryopreserved, but we felt fragile and bruised by the failure. This disappointment and heartache coupled with trying to deal with the grief and despair of missing Rosie meant I had no option other than to put the idea of having a baby out of my mind for now. I continued with counselling, but David didn't feel able to articulate his despair to a counsellor.

Over the next months, David would come home from work and head straight out to the gym. He became more obsessive about personal fitness and shed five stone but was even more distant and unwilling to communicate.

On my return to dance teaching and running the school, I threw myself into training our young dancers. Surrounding myself with talented kids and putting on shows brought structure and optimism to my days.

It would be a whole year before we were able to have another attempt with Sam's one remaining frozen embryo.

Rosie's Charity Broadens Its Services
July 2005

Meanwhile Rosie's Rainbow was going from strength to strength. So, I invested a lot of time and dedication into the running of Rosie's Rainbow Fund as well as teaching at the school. The charity was expanding and our work at John Radcliffe proving very successful. The urgent need for our services led to the decision to offer music therapy at two more hospitals.

In addition to our work at John Radcliffe Hospital, the trustees and I set up music therapy at Royal Berks Hospital in Reading, where we implemented weekly music sessions in the Lion and Dolphin children's wards. Many of the children from John Radcliffe also had treatment at Royal Berks, so this was a natural progression. This was closely followed by adding music therapy at Stoke Mandeville Hospital in Aylesbury. Children were desperately needing support in the children's spinal unit, where incapacitated kids had been in-patients for months.

The trustees and I had a very clear vision for taking Rosie's Rainbow forward. We now had a fantastic service running for the children, but what about the parents?

The hospital was still full of frightened and stressed parents enduring the same fear and loneliness I had encountered. There must be a way we could support these mums and dads at such a difficult time.

Helene introduced us to her friend Amanda, an experienced aromatherapist who also had many years of training and a wealth of knowledge about care for parents from her years as a midwife in the NHS. Her knowledge and compassionate manner were perfect for the new role we created at John Radcliffe.

Amanda offered a unique service. Her holistic aromatherapy massage sessions provided a much-needed time-out for parents. While a nurse would watch over their child, parents would be allowed a small window of time away to unwind and destress with powerful natural aromatherapy oils. Amanda also provided a listening ear in a confidential space where very frightened parents could offload and renew their energy. Her sessions became a lifeline for so many, and testimonials and thank you letters from grateful parents flooded in.

We now had a specially designated space in the brand-new hospital at John Radcliffe. I was relieved that the drab old ward 4B in the bleak old hospital block had gone and been replaced by the much improved bright and shiny children's hospital. Due to very generous funding from the Bach trust, we proudly added a gold door plaque to our two rooms which bore the name *Rosie's Rainbow Therapy Room*. There were now designated wards for different illnesses, and whether parents had children in the oncology ward, the surgical, adolescent, or craniofacial wards, we looked after all of them. Amanda had a long waiting list each week, so Christine and the play team would prioritise the neediest to benefit from her sessions. Amanda's midwifery experience was also invaluable to parents who had just given birth. She supported these new mums who were not only nursing sick babies but also dealing with their own postpartum difficulties.

The jobs of music therapist and parent support therapist were so rewarding for our team, seeing happy children and re-energised, calmed parents. At the very least these mums and dads had a sympathetic listening ear. Sadly, many also had to deal with the heartbreak of bereavement. Over the years, our Rosie's Rainbow team have been there for thousands of parents at the worst possible time in their lives. I felt that some good had come about from the fear and loneliness I experienced whilst there with Rosie.

Jenni Thomas, who had been instrumental in providing bereavement support to me, was now on board and heading up our dedicated bereavement team as well as agreeing to become a patron of the charity. Experience with child bereavement and running her own charity meant there was nobody more qualified nor better able to help than Jenni. Through Rosie's Rainbow, other parents were now able to access her care and support. Some of these bereaved parents had lost children at John Radcliffe and so these were immediate referrals, but many pleas for support were also flooding in from devastated parents who had lost their beloved children in every dreadful scenario you could imagine from suicides, drownings, premature baby loss, to sudden illness or fatal accidents. The shock and disbelief that there were so many of us out there needing help never left me. Jenni and our team of compassionate therapists were a lifesaver. Child loss is not something you ever *get over*, but we were able to walk beside mums with true empathy and understanding so no one needed to cope with this terrible grief alone.

Alongside the charity's development, Helene's daughter Ella was becoming increasingly unwell. Issues resulting from Rett syndrome were progressively worsening and little Ella was suffering breathing difficulties and seizures. She was attending a school for children with special needs and Helene was spending longer periods with Ella in and out of hospital. Shockingly she had a life-limiting prognosis, and it was the cruellest twist of fate that one of my oldest and dearest friends and her family would at some point have to face a similar outcome to ours. Helene and Mike were doing all they could for Ella, but it was clear that her chest infections were becoming more frequent and difficult to manage.

Remembering how Rosie, her sister, and friends had raised money for Ella back in 2002 just before Rosie became ill and Rosie's heartfelt unscripted speech at the end of their fundraising show *Forever and A Day*, it was very clear to myself and the trustees that we should offer music in schools for children with special needs like Ella. Helene was very active within Ella's special needs school and so the charity purchased some sound beds for Ella and her friends to enjoy. They were delivered to the school and the children were able to lie down and respond to the sounds and vibrations through the beds even though many of them were unable to talk.

We instigated regular Rosie's Rainbow music sessions in four special needs schools. The singers in Rosie's Rainbow Choir would visit the schools on many occasions, and we encouraged all the children with varying disabilities to share instruments and sing and dance together with our performers. It was a very easy partnership. The choir would gain as much from these collaborations as the young recipients and a happy and productive time was had by all.

The special schools benefitted from the wonderful teaching of Pauline Burr, a gifted teacher and composer of children's songs. This delightful lady had the extraordinary ability to churn out hundreds of catchy melodies and tunes at the drop of a rainbow-coloured hat. She had recorded a series of very successful children's songs on CD which for many years she sold through the Early Learning Centre. She was able to write perfect songs on varying themes to complement the school curriculum. We would witness Pauline's enchanting sessions with admiration and the children clearly reaped so much joy from these. She would encourage severely disabled children to move and even dance to her music. In the words of one little girl with severe cerebral palsy, "Rosie's Rainbow makes me very, very happy when we sing to the lovely, lovely music."

Pauline and our team were ready to embark on our new initiative offering music to pre-school children with special needs. We ran Rosie's Rainbow Fund Mini Music Makers sessions in a bright and comfortable location in Thame.

It became very clear that the parents of these little children were still in shock, trying to adapt to the fact that their children had complex needs of varying degrees. Their lives had changed radically since they were expecting their babies. They had to adjust to all the problems entailed in raising a child who would possibly never do many of the things they had dreamed of. Mini Music Makers was full of laughter and music. Pauline, with her acoustic guitar, was a perfect match for these gentle sessions for the littlest ones and their mums. We filled a big prop box full of rainbow-coloured scarves, rattles, props, and instruments. Every small child was warmly welcomed, and their names added to Pauline's 'Hello' song. We offered regular coffee and homemade cakes after each session and the parents were able to connect with each other, which made them feel less alone. Each of these new initiatives fell into place as though they had always been there. Rosie was truly working her magic from her rainbow.

We ran a multitude of fundraising events to bring in much-needed money for the services we were providing. These took a great deal of planning and effort from the trustees, but we also had a lot of fun. We did everything from balls to bingo nights, shows, outdoor events, and fairs. Awareness was spreading and schools and local businesses became involved and ran their own events. Rosie's Rainbow Choir toured local clubs, pubs, and theatres and appeared on radio and TV. There were magazine features and newspaper stories. I was asked to speak at public events and to the media. It was always a strange feeling giving speeches in public. Oddly I always managed to speak about Rosie and the charity and remain totally in control. My acting training stood me in good stead. It was as though I had a professional front where I could talk succinctly and articulately about Rosie and her story. There was a marked difference between the confident public image and the bereaved grieving mess who would drive home afterwards, feeling wrung out and overcome with sadness. However, I was so proud of Rosie and needed to ensure she remained centre stage and felt she was there pushing me through it, feeding me my lines while I was there as her channel, allowing her to speak and work through me.

Painful Reminders
November 2005

Although Ellie had plans to audition for dance college and to move to London, we felt it was too premature. She had endured two years of hell since losing her sister and was not emotionally ready to cope with the tough regime of dance school. So, she joined Redroofs student course, which we thought would be a good halfway house, allowing her some growing-up time before she finally spread her wings and left home. I had to admit it was also a relief for us to know that she would not be flying the nest just yet, and now six weeks into the term, she had settled smoothly into a new routine on the musical theatre course with a group of friendly students.

Even with Ellie still living at home, it was becoming harder to be in our house. I could no longer even go into Rosie's bedroom. Her room was directly at the top of the stairs, and I was faced with the problem every time I went up. We hadn't moved anything in her room for over two years, and it was just as she had left it, and yet had she lived she would have changed the room around. It would have been the room of Rosie the young teenager, but of course this could never be. Turning the room into something else was not the answer either, but I never wanted it to become a shrine. Keeping the door firmly shut, I looked the other way whenever I reached the landing.

Rosie's magnolia tree with her ashes beneath it confronted me each time I looked out of the windows at the back of the house. I wished we had considered a more subtle place for her tree, but we hadn't, and now it was causing me a great deal of pain. I could see Rosie sitting at the top of the stairs having a strop when we were already ten minutes late for school and refusing to let me brush her hair. "Rosie," I would be on a short fuse, "for heaven's sake get in the car right now!" Ellie, knowing she needed to step in, would cajole her, and eventually I would hear giggling coming from upstairs. Then Rosie would appear with her hair all brushed into a ballet bun by Ellie, and the girls would grab their school bags, jump into the car, the nonsense swiftly dissipated as they sang show songs in full throttle all the way to school.

Even turning into our drive became an issue as I was haunted by the image of her getting in the car for the last ever drive back to John Radcliffe.

Flashes and fragments of our past life were everywhere. Rosie dictating poems to me as she messed about in the bath. Rosie and Ellie adorning our old cats Doodle and Daisy in coloured ribbons and, with Lucy and Laura, parading them around the house on our old gold metal trolley like a carnival float.

There were flashbacks of Rosie whichever way I turned, with agonising reminders of all that we had lost. For my mental well-being I knew that the best thing would be to move somewhere new, where we could start over and pack some of the difficult memories into boxes, where we did not have them staring at us every day.

To my surprise David agreed that it would be best for us all to have a new start. I hoped that a move may also restore our relationship.

So, we put the house on the market, and in early 2006 it was sold.

Rosie's belongings were stacked into large brown packing cases. I was not ready to part with anything, so her entire wardrobe came with us. David and his brothers stoically dug up the casket of Rosie's ashes and moved it with the purple magnolia tree into a shady spot at the corner of Mum's garden. It was an agonising thing to do, but we couldn't leave Rosie behind. Once it was done, we knew it had been the right choice. Mum was only too happy to accommodate it. The tree burst into flower a few months later with glorious purple flowers.

We moved to a bright modern house near the River Thames. The change of environment was healing, and the airy house just what we needed. Life felt more settled at last. Ellie had a room on the top floor, which she loved. There was a light, bright empty bedroom at the end of the landing. Standing in there alone one day when David had gone to work and Ellie was out, I looked around and, in my mind's eye, imagined a cot, with the room decorated with Peter Rabbit curtains and accessories. Maybe it was nearly time to have another attempt at IVF.

Meanwhile ,with a growing interest in spirituality, I went to a mystic fair at Olympia with Helene's husband Mike. He was also fascinated with all things spiritual and when we arrived, he left to go in search of healing crystals. While he was gone I had quite an extraordinary reading with a well-known medium called Betty Palko. Having read for Princess Diana, the queue for readings was long. After waiting in line for an hour, I met Betty. Like the other mediums I had visited, she told me she saw a baby. It was mine, she thought. I said I was almost fifty. She just shrugged and smiled and said stranger things had happened and she was just telling me what she was being told from spirit. Yet another person predicting another child. I prayed she may be right this time. She also described seeing me writing, and that I was possibly going to be in the media.

Rosie Yes X
May 2006

Mia Dolan was a psychic medium who had tragically lost her son. She had written a book in which she described so clearly her belief that all our children continue to live and flourish on the other side. I was desperate to contact her for a reading. My logical mind told me to be sensible, there was hardly any chance she would reply, but I was aching for a message from Rosie.

Driving home from Alfie's walk, I was thinking how much I was missing my daughter and wishing someone as good as Mia Dolan could give me a reading when suddenly a car pulled out in front of me. The number plate was *MIA*. I thought it was amusing and shrugged it off, but then another car pulled out. The number plate read *RO51 YSX*.

Like Rosie – yes – kiss!

That was my cue. Back home I found Mia's email address at the back of her paperback and emailed asking for a reading, saying I had lost a daughter but not giving any further details. She probably received loads of letters and requests for readings, but I sent it anyway! Two days later I received an email from Mia Dolan with her phone number, saying to call her but to keep the number to myself or she would be swamped with calls. So, I telephoned Mia for a reading and set a date to go to the Isle of Sheppey at the end of May.

David agreed to drive me to her house. It was a two-hour drive to Sheerness. Approaching the town, I could feel the atmosphere of the place. Dingy, out of date, and run down, a bleak seafront, a few kids playing in a sand pit, a couple sitting on the seafront deep in conversation.

We passed a run-down-looking nightclub dubiously called Tantras and a scruffy amusement arcade which was shut. David thought the town looked shabby, but to me it was magical because now it was not just a description in her book; it was the real place.

We found Mia's house easily, so I suggested we find somewhere for a coffee as we had arrived early.

We pulled up in a deserted seafront car park, where we quickly realised that a good cup of coffee would be an impossibility and settled for a McDonald's, buying coffee and a doughnut which I couldn't finish. We had a brief walk along the beach, where I found a seashell which I stuffed into my handbag.

"Don't ask me to come in" had been David's mantra all the way down the M25. He didn't want to know, or he was spooked by the thought of it. So, at five minutes to twelve, I passed a group of local kids sitting on the wall outside their house. I sensed them nudging one another, whispering, "There goes another one!" Wishing they hadn't seen me, I knocked on the door of the end house. It was an ordinary 1930s property in an ordinary road, but this was not an ordinary day, and everything seemed surreal.

Mia opened the door straight away. She was a tall, blonde, motherly-looking woman with a round sunny face, the darkest blue eyes, and a welcoming openness which I warmed to immediately. I followed her through to the kitchen. In the corner was a small square table with a yellow plastic tablecloth, on which sat a battered old tape recorder, a small candle, and a pack of cigarettes. She offered me a cup of coffee, spooning in several teaspoons of powdered milk from a jar. All the while she chatted away as though she had known me forever, and any nerves I had dissolved along with the Mellow Birds coffee. She pulled the blind down, laughing, and told me that the neighbouring kids were convinced she was a witch and would point at her through the window. She lit her cigarette, exhaled a long puff of smoke, and the reading began.

"Okay, so we are going to start with a health scan, then what I call a floater." This, she explained, was a state in which she would receive random images in her head. "Then we will go on to your finances, relationships, and the rest. I can't guarantee that Rosie will come through and I'm certainly not going to pretend."

Straight away she told me I had a purple aura along with pink, green, and a lot of blue as well. The pink showed stress, she explained, and the blue indicated I was someone who liked to be in control. Then, the purple. "Purple is wonderful. It means you are a sensitive. In time you will learn to develop your psychic ability. You will be a healer. And I see a date, the 5th. I think it must be June 5th. On that date something will happen, and this is going to be the beginning of something great for you." She stared past me and over my left shoulder, almost never at me. My health was good. From the head down she said I had a small sinus problem. Also, she picked up an issue with my bite and that a dentist visit should be arranged, stiffness at the back of the neck, tension in the shoulders, some lower back problems, a slightly irritated bowel, and weak lower abdominal muscles which needed strengthening. Moving down, she said I would get a bad knee and sore feet, but generally not to worry about anything. She saw me walking beside water (I walked Alfie by the river). She saw us doing a small plumbing job, "…nothing major, maybe a leaky tap but certainly not a flood."

David drove me home, seemingly content to listen to my excited ramblings and a full report of all she had predicted while he had sat in the car outside her house. I left the Isle of Sheppey with an even firmer belief in the afterlife, a feeling of overwhelming gratitude, and a seashell which took up residence in my purse to prove to myself it had really happened. Later that evening when we got home, Shirley came online to ask whether David would fix her leaky tap when we went there a few days later!

Discovering Reiki
June 2006

Needing to have some time out from the last few hectic months teaching and moving house, Helene and I snatched a weekend spa break. It was just what we needed, and we readily succumbed to lolling around in white dressing gowns, lazing by the pool with a magazine, and enjoying healthy fresh food.

I had my first full body massage almost as soon as I arrived and afterwards found the tranquillity room empty. It was dark and smelled of calming aromatherapy herbs. There were warm stone beds, twinkly lights in the darkened ceiling, and fluffy towels. Drawn to the peace and quiet, I chose a warm bed in the corner. Suddenly and unexpectedly, I was crying my eyes out. I couldn't stop the tears and didn't try. The floodgates opened and there were torrential tears over the next two days.

Then I discovered reiki for the first time. Because it sounded relaxing and was new to me, I booked a session. I knew nothing about reiki. The therapist was a reiki master and she explained that reiki was a form of alternative healing. This Japanese healing system transfers universal energy, either 'hands on' or 'hands off', through the palms, with often profound effects and the ability to promote physical and emotional healing.

After laying on her treatment bed, she switched on some calming pan pipes music. She was not even touching me, but I slipped into a trance-like state and the sensation was so odd. I was seeing fleeting images, almost like a black and white movie or one of those old-fashioned zoetropes which created the impression of early silent movie animations. I could see eagles with huge wing spans, mountains, and faces, although I did not recognise many of them. As soon as I tried to decipher them, they disappeared.

I could sense she was moving her hands up and down above my body. As she moved, I felt hot then cold and then as if there was a massive weight on my chest so could hardly breathe. In fact, I looked up to see if she was bearing down on my chest and ask her to stop pressing so hard. Surprisingly her hands were nowhere near, and her eyes were closed. Afterwards she told me I was very blocked around the stomach area and that it was grief all being stored there. She had worked on releasing the negative energy.

When the healing ended, I felt totally exhausted but also as if a huge weight had lifted. I asked her whether she thought it would benefit me to enrol on a course to learn how to do reiki. She replied, "You don't have to worry about finding a course, as it will find you. In other words, when the pupil is ready, the teacher appears!"

I came home spaced out but calm and hopeful that I could find out more about reiki and other holistic therapies. Flicking through a magazine the next afternoon, I stumbled upon a local reiki course and immediately booked to start on June 5th, the exact date Mia Dolan had referred to.

The reiki course opened my eyes to another world, where I discovered the ability to see aura, meet my spirit guides, and learn so much about the afterlife. During the training I had some of the weirdest experiences. The teacher had led us into a meditation where we were to meet with our reiki guide. I was panicking and thinking I would be the only one in the room who would see absolutely nothing. He kept saying to us to stop trying so hard and to just be. Suddenly I saw my guide! I thought first that I was working very hard to create someone so that I would not feel stupid, but then he just appeared. It was as though a veil was lifting, revealing a tall North American Indian with chieftain feathers on his head. His face was as clear to me as if he was in the same room and no more than a few inches away. I could see smooth brown skin and a slightly hooked nose. He was standing beside a waterfall and beneath him was rushing water. He looked directly at me. I stared then turned away and then looked again to see if I was dreaming, and there I saw Rosie. She was kneeling by his side. She was not doing much, but she was there, wearing a soft blue dress and smiling. I asked him his name, which he told me. It sounded like an American Indian sort of name. I heard the teacher saying to us, "Now ask your guide a question."

In my head I asked him, "Is Rosie with you?"

In a deep voice, his reply was immediate: "She is with me, but she is also with you." Then he vanished, and I was back in the room at the hall in Gerrards Cross!

The whole experience had a profound effect on me. I qualified in my Stage 1 and 2 reiki, achieving a healing diploma. I sensed this was a significant development in my spiritual journey. My ongoing need to connect with Rosie was leading me on a voyage of discovery. Firstly, I was approaching this new world with some trepidation, but as I learned more, I realised there was nothing to be afraid of and that our loved ones had never left us. They walk beside us always and are close by.

It had become a regular source of comfort to read books about the afterlife and I was already attending the local spiritualist church on an almost weekly basis. I was developing an awareness, learning so much, and practising reiki on family and friends. My spiritual growth uplifted me some of the time. Our school was busy, and Rosie's Rainbow Fund was doing well. Doing my best not to dwell too much on our failure with IVF, it remained on the back burner.

Lucy and The X Factor
June 2006

Lucy Benjamin performs

"Hi, Carolyn, I need to talk to you." It was Lucy Benjamin on the phone. She sounded flustered but excited.

"Listen, I must be bloody mad, but I have agreed to compete on ITV's *The X Factor: Battle of the Stars*. I can't even believe I have agreed to do this. But anyway, I am, and if by any chance I win, which I won't, I am nominating Rosie's Rainbow Fund. Don't get too excited. I will be knocked out on the first round, I'm sure."

"Wow, Lucy, you are so brave. That's amazing. Gosh, thank you, I am so honoured. Rosie will be right beside you," I said. We had to keep it a secret until it was promoted by ITV. Once it was announced on the media, word spread rapidly. I promised Lucy that if she got through to the quarter final, we would be there if we could get tickets for the live shows.

Lucy was such a perfectionist and had a huge capacity for work, and she entered this epic TV show against some tough competition. To add to the challenge, she had confided to me that she was pregnant and not only feeling nauseous but was actually being sick and had a bucket backstage. She gave it her all, however, and we watched her sing brilliantly. On the very first night, Sharon Osbourne let it slip that Lucy was pregnant, so the secret was out. My heart was in my mouth watching her, and what blew my mind that first night was that the whole country now knew about Rosie's Rainbow. Once again, although Rosie was not physically there, she very much was.

On the second night we found out that every phone vote secured 10p for the charity. This could really be something amazing if she kept this up. The phone rang literally all day long and there were press interviews where I was asked about Lucy's involvement with Rosie's Rainbow Fund, and I had to explain how she was an ex-pupil and now a patron and all about the charity's work. I felt heady and proud, loving the attention on Rosie.

Lucy went through to the next round again the following evening and Louis Walsh said that the reason she stayed in the show that day was because of her charity. Louis saying this in front of thousands of viewers made me tingle with pride and feel as high as a kite. I knew with no doubt that Rosie was right there beside Lucy and still centre stage.

People watching the show were calling us and offering to donate and fundraise. A music teacher from Windsor was going to give us all her holiday class money, and a mobile recycling company offered to donate all their money from old mobiles. It was a reminder that there were so many good people in the world.

As Lucy went through to yet another round, Mum, Sam, and I were asked to do a full interview about Redroofs, Lucy's old drama school. That night Lucy went through to the live shows. The Great British public were loving Lucy and she arranged tickets for us to the first live show at Wembley. It was slightly alarming to think how much Rosie's Rainbow stood to make if Lucy continued to win the rounds.

Attending the live show at Wembley was awesome. David and I took Ellie, our music therapist Ceridwen, and her daughter. It seemed so surreal that Lucy was talking about Rosie to thousands of people in the audience and to millions of viewers from all over the world. She sang like a star, and I was in awe of her. She was not only gifted but also had a heart of gold.

On a more depressing note, the day after the first live show, Helene's daughter Ella was admitted back in Wycombe Hospital again. It was the familiar scenario with a chest infection then seizures and high fever. I went to visit Helene and Ella. It was always hard going into the ward. Seeing Ella's arm bound up to hide the cannulas made my flesh creep and brought back painful memories.

The play specialist there was interested in the idea of music therapy, and I suggested that the charity bought some musical toys for the children on the ward.

On June 7th, 2006, Lucy went through to the finals of ITV's *The X Factor: Battle of the Stars*. We were reeling from the whole thing. Since we couldn't have tickets for the show, we decided to throw an impromptu party on the night of the *X Factor* final. It had started as a request from Ceridwen that could she come along to our place and watch it together? This escalated into one hell of a party. We collected thirty of our family and friends, who congregated at our house to watch and cheer Lucy on. Everyone brought nibbles, food, and drink and the atmosphere was electric.

Niki, my sister-in-law, had flown down from Edinburgh specially to join us and told the cabin crew all about Lucy and Rosie's Rainbow Fund. They made an announcement to everyone on the plane asking them to vote. Mum came, along with Sam and the family, Ceridwen with her daughter and partner, Helene came with the family, including Ella, who thankfully had been discharged from hospital the day before. Mike too, and all of David's brothers and their families. Shirley, Rosie's nurse, said she would not miss it for the world, and we also had a bunch of Ellie's very excited friends.

Voting that night reached fever pitch. With 10p from every phone call going to Rosie's Rainbow Fund, our phone bills became astronomical, but no one cared. Squashed together on sofas or cross-legged on the floor in front of the large television in our living room, eyes glued to the screen, mobiles in one hand and a wine glass in the other, we waited for the winner to be announced. The screams which filled our house when Lucy was announced winner of ITV's *The X Factor: Battle of the Stars* were probably heard not just by our neighbours but all over Berkshire. Stunned, all I could think was oh my God, this is beyond the realms of the imagination and how wonderful, but at the same time, how could this be happening when Rosie wasn't there? Or was she? I didn't know whether to laugh or cry. Both Ceridwen and Shirley spotted me wiping away tears and held me up both physically and mentally. This possibly felt like the best party we had ever had.

Phil arrived armed with his filming equipment and made a video recording of our evening, which we sent to Lucy and our friends. It ended with a thank you from me for all she has done for us, a massive heartfelt thank you for giving Rosie a voice and for all her efforts. I don't think my thanks were enough, but what do you say to someone who has told six million viewers every night for a week about the work being carried out in memory of the most beloved daughter and sister in the world?

We realised that the profile of Rosie's Rainbow Fund had soared and that six million viewers now knew of Rosie, so for me, knowing our beautiful girl was still working her magic kept me high as a kite all week.

The following day there were non-stop calls from press and TV. I did two television interviews for local news stations, talking fluently about our incredible win, our daughter's entire story, and what it meant to me and to Rosie's Rainbow Fund. It was like talking about some other person's child. I managed to stay focussed although exhausted.

Lucy rang me next day while I was out in town shopping. "This is top secret," she said. "You have to swear not to say anything yet, but listen, the executive producer has allowed me to telephone you before telling the rest of the country. The public votes have won Rosie's Rainbow Fund £147,000!"

Our Second Attempt at IVF
August 2006

After a year as a Redroofs student, Ellie decided the time was right to embark on a new path and successfully auditioned for a dance course at a London dance college. She would be starting her new adventure in September, leaving home and us! She had a boyfriend, also called David, but we called him little David to avoid confusion. Little David also chose the same college, and so they went together. It was good for her at that time since he had known Rosie well, and he understood Ellie. I was pleased that she had someone to look out for her.

It was two whole years since the first failed IVF attempt. After consulting David, we now felt able to cope with another try. I drove to the Lister Hospital on my own. It was odd to be back there again. The nurse advised that this time it would only take about a week and a half from the day I started the process to the embryo implant day. I had to give this my best shot. If it didn't work, I would survive. Somehow, I had made it through the last two years. This time I kept it private and didn't share it with many people.

On Chelsea Bridge I tried to remain calm and detached, despite being very nervous. From my vantage point, I could see the familiar brown hospital building over the water. Taking a deep breath, I walked purposefully to the hospital entrance and entered the assisted conception unit. Nothing had changed. The same receptionist was stationed behind her desk. She ran her eyes down the list. "Your appointment doesn't seem to be in the book." My heart thumped. "If you take a seat and wait, I will try and find out what has happened," she said.

The waiting area was still the same with all the familiar notices on the wall. Two veiled women sat opposite, next to their husbands. A stressed lady burst into tears as I sat there. She fumbled in her bag for tissues and mopped her eyes behind her glasses while her husband patted her on the leg. I tried to imagine her scenario and wondered if she had lost a child too, or whether she was just unable to conceive.

Eventually after a two-hour wait, it was my turn.

On the scan table the nurse was prodding about and looking at a screen beside the bed. "You have a cyst on your ovary. It might clear itself or it might not, so you will need to wait and see, and we can plan the best course of action and treatment. We will be giving you a prescription, but first your case will have to be brought to a meeting tomorrow because you are now fifty-two!"

"Fifty-one," I corrected her.

"The thing is," she said, "we don't generally treat women over fifty, so we need the go-ahead from the doctors." My heart was racing, and I felt like crying.

All my plans for keeping calm and controlled were evaporating. I had no recollection of anyone mentioning this to me. Back in 2004 when I asked for the embryo to be frozen, no one said that once I was fifty years old, it would be useless. They told me I could use it for up to five years. It had only been in the freezer for two, so what was the problem?

I left the building feeling gutted and upset and phoned Sam. She was on holiday in Devon, and I felt guilty for calling but had to tell someone. I was confused about them storing eggs and now being told that I was too old. I had understood the age of the egg donor was important, not the recipient, and Sam was thirty-eight at the time. They had told me there was no hurry and I would be able to use them any time in the next five years. I had paid the facility for five years of embryo freezing, so how was that appropriate if they knew I couldn't use them?

Two days later and feeling very anxious, I finally received a call from one of the nurses. "I expect you have been worried sick, haven't you?" I was on edge but controlled myself, knowing they had to follow protocol and they were only going through a process, and anyway, Ellie was home for the holidays and sitting beside me. So, I replied sweetly, "Yes, just a bit worried!"

She continued, "Well, we had the meeting, and the result is you can go ahead provided you make an appointment with one of the doctors so they can point out all the implications of being an older pregnant woman."

I said, "Right, that's fine," wanting to vent but didn't as Ellie was listening in.

I realised how stressed I had been about it, despite doing my best to think of other things. After the call, Ellie and I spent a lovely afternoon shopping in Reading followed by a pleasant pizza lunch.

Pregnancy and birth for women over fifty was certainly becoming more commonplace. Data showed that in 2002, out of ninety-six women over fifty, twenty-four gave birth to live babies and each year the figure was increasing. My inner voice asked if I could go through with this. The answer was yes, but I questioned whether I was even more determined because of all the psychic predictions. Was I doing it to prove that there really was an afterlife? If this was true, then Rosie was not dead in the spiritual sense and was conducting operations from her rainbow, where she was waiting for me. If there was no baby, then that meant there was no life after death, and I would never see her again even in the next life. On the more practical side, we had this beautiful new house and I wanted to fill it with those normal family sort of sounds much missed over the last two and a half years, and of course I wanted a cot in that room. Remembering how ill I became last time around, I knew I must do everything I could to stay well. So, I rested and had a couple of reiki treatments.

The Lister Hospital invited me for an internal scan first thing on Friday, September 1st. Liz, the IVF nurse, chatted about my embryo whilst she conducted the scan.

"There's only one whole one left," I said. She surprised me with her reply.

"A whole one is possibly all you will need. If the conditions are right, then there is no reason why it should not implant successfully, resulting in a pregnancy."

"But I only have the one and I know the rate of success after thawing is vastly reduced and because it's only one, it may not work. Have you ever seen just one embryo turn into a baby?"

"Absolutely I have!" she said cheerily.

That was all I needed to hear. I smiled gratefully at her. "Positive thoughts," she said.

Dr Pareekh, the consultant, greeted me after the scan and presented me with a lengthy list of risks of both being pregnant and of giving birth at fifty-two. Miscarriage, diabetes, stroke, and high blood pressure even before the birth. At birth there was the possibility of complications resulting in a Caesarean section, postpartum haemorrhage, and the need for blood transfusion. The list was gruesome and more extensive than I had previously expected.

Dr Pareekh continued, "I am sure you have researched this, and you know what this entails. There isn't a problem with us carrying this out as long as you are fully aware, but we have a duty to point all these risks out to you. If you were starting from scratch, we would not be able to treat you as you are over the age limit, but as we already have your frozen embryo, there is no reason why we cannot go ahead."

"You can see my point," I said. "How can I possibly leave a potential child in a freezer?"

"Of course, of course," she answered. "As long as you realise the success rate is small, only 9–10%," she added. "But anyway, I wish you luck."

A couple of weeks later on September 13th, I moved onto the next stage of the treatment. The process was the same as the last round.

It was all a bit scary, but I was in a very different head space this time and therefore able to cope with a *Not Pregnant* sign on the pregnancy test!

The tablets made me feel sick. Annoyingly pounds of weight were piling on and I hoped it was just the tablets, but my scales showed I had gained three pounds in less than two weeks. Other than that, I remained as detached as possible from the treatment, keeping myself busy with getting the Redroofs school year underway.

It was September 26th, and a new nurse was conducting the scans. She was interested to know whether I had children. I felt the lump in my throat as I relayed my story yet again. She was shocked, turning very quiet. "I can't imagine what that must be like. The loss of a child is just so terrible. If anything happened to my two boys, I couldn't survive it!"

"We do not get to choose," I replied. "You never think in a million years it will happen to you, but you do have to learn to cope with it."

"Were your two children natural births?" she asked.

"Oh yes, two perfectly normal, natural ones."

In my uncompromising position on the scan table, I could see she was attempting to absorb my sad situation.

She said gently, "I am pleased to say your lining is lovely and thick. It is somewhere between 10.4 and 12. That is perfect, and we can now sort out a thaw date. But you know you can never replace your lost child. Do you feel you can maybe begin to heal with the promise of a new life?"

"All I can say is that I have to try, and I can't leave the possibility in a freezer."

Wishing me luck, she sent me to wait in the waiting room. I was feeling choked by this time and wondered how I would cope and hold back tears if anyone said anything. Eventually a nurse arrived and ushered me into a side room. "We will thaw your embryo on Thursday, September 28th." My heart pounded. "Have your final nasal spray tonight and start the Cyclogest tomorrow. If it all goes well, then we will have you in for the embryo transfer this Friday, the 29th."

"So, what are the chances of a successful defrost?" I am not sure where her information came from, but it was apparently 14%, which was a disappointing statistic.

"But if it survives the thaw, then we are in with a chance. It will mean it is a strong embryo," she said. She promised to call me on Thursday the 28th. I wondered how I would keep calm till then, knowing that if the embryo dies off in the thawing process, then all my hopes would finally be gone. I left the hospital with my stomach somewhere in my throat. Now that push had come to shove, it was frightening, and all my old nerves and anxiety returned, but determined to stay calm I whispered the reiki chant all the way back to the car.

Sam sounded matter of fact on the phone and said it was beyond my control and I would now have to wait and see.

In the morning I went to the dentist and my stomach churned all the way to the appointment. I could not work out whether it was dental nerves and jitters or the realisation that my embryo had only one more day on ice before its future was decided. I wondered whether its fate was already mapped out though. Sam said she believed that everything is pre-ordained, and if it is meant to be, then it will be.

She thought we were just vehicles for whatever fate ordained for us, and that since Ellie was now eighteen and might soon have children, I would have grandchildren. For all her common sense and steadfast love and support, she could not fully relate to my circumstances. She had her two healthy children and therefore could never truly appreciate how hard it is to have to survive being left with one. There was no point in my getting frustrated with her attitude. As close as she was to Rosie, hers was the view of an aunt and not a mother.

I threw myself into work with a frantic desperation to keep busy. I taught tap classes all afternoon, managed to deal with the mail, and ordered up a set of new Rainbow Choir outfits. Now it was all in the hands of fate.

Val's text message that evening was, *It's better to regret the things you have done than the things you have not!*

September 28th was embryo thaw day, the beginning of a new and exciting adventure or the end of the road. If it really was the dead end, I would need to find another way of moving forward.

For the next few hours, I visualised my embryo as a little cartoon baby surrounded in a purple light. He was sitting there in a little white nappy, waving at me. By mid-morning, I was totally beside myself with the tension, so I spent the next hour trying to get through to the hospital, making numerous calls with no answer. Finally, I had a voicemail from one of the IVF nurses asking me to ring her back as our calls had crossed.

By that time, I had to drive to Redroofs to teach my tap classes. I was completely distracted and unable to concentrate on timesteps and shuffle pick-ups. The only 'pick up' I could think of was picking up the phone. However, another call came during a tap class, and I dashed outside to answer it.

"Is that Carolyn Mayling? We thawed your one embryo today and it was successful and survived very well. We would like you in here tomorrow morning at 11.20am for the embryo transfer." I breathed a massive sigh of relief!

The stress physically melted away, and I felt light, bright, and very hungry. I called David straight away, then Sam. I was over the moon and could hardly believe it. This was only stage one, but I felt thrilled and hopeful.

On September 29th, embryo transfer day dawned bright and sunny. Waking at 5am, I spent the next hour practising reiki and preparing myself for the implant. I imagined beams of soft purple light and lots of warmth surrounding my little embryo, a bit like a room makeover – soft lights and underfloor heating. The perfect ambience and a good place to hang out!

The M4 was clear, David was in a calm mood, and we arrived in London in good time. Driving along the embankment in the direction of Battersea Bridge, I crossed my fingers and prayed this might be our lucky day.

The receptionist ticked me on her list, and we took a seat in the familiar waiting room. "You must have a full bladder, but go slowly with the water. Not sure how long you may have to wait! Good luck," she said.

As before, David wanted to sit in the waiting room while I went to the transfer room. "You have been here before, haven't you?" the nurse asked.

"Yes," I said.

"Were you lucky?"

"No!"

"Well, maybe this time you will be."

I wondered how many ladies had been successful since I was last here. A face appeared at the hatch in that now familiar wall. "Hi, I am Sophie, and I am looking after your embryo today."

Bless her, I thought, my embryo's nanny!

There were brisk footsteps outside, and Dr Pareekh appeared, smiling brightly and looking ready for business.

"Well, the embryo has made it, which is lovely. And not only is it surviving well, but it is also still dividing, which is a very good sign. It is obviously a real little fighter."

I said, "It was so nerve-wracking yesterday waiting to hear the news."

"I am not in the least surprised," said Dr Pareekh as she positioned herself at the end of the bed to begin the procedure.

Sophie popped her head through the hatch and pointed out the embryo on the monitor. It looked just the same as the ones from the first time. Soon the embryo was handed through the hatch to Dr Pareekh, and she deftly put it in place with a syringe. After all the weeks of treatment, this was the quick and painless part. "Just take it a little easy and in two weeks you do the test."

As we drove home, David came out with another of his one-liners:

"Well, the embryo will either say *I fuckin' like it in here* or it will say *I'm fuckin' out of here!*"

Not a man of eloquent words, but that pretty much summed it up in a womb-shaped nutshell!

Looking at the calendar two weeks from the transfer to work out the date for the pregnancy test, I was shocked to see it was Friday, October 13th. Maybe I would do the test on the 14th or even the 12th!

We had seats for the musical *Wicked*, which had just opened in town. Helene, who came along with us, kept whispering at me to stop rubbing my stomach. My embryo attended his first show. We were all totally absorbed and swept along by Idina Menzel's extraordinary performance. Every few minutes, I kept thinking oh my God, there is now a potential new member of my family inside me.

A few days later I began looking for symptoms. I was very tired and sleeping a bit during the day, which was unlike me, but it had been a stressful week. Val said that she had no signs this early on. I couldn't stop thinking about the possibilities. It was foolish. I didn't want to be sad and disappointed like the last time but was feeling increasingly anxious. As usual, teaching and carrying out our necessary charity jobs kept me focussed.

That week I made a trip to John Radcliffe Hospital for a charity meeting. The sight of the old building to the side of the new children's hospital still made me go cold even after four years.

In the week leading up to taking the predictor test, I was feeling sick. Was it the tablets, or was something happening inside? Unable to resist the temptation any longer, I went to Boots, bought the pregnancy test, took it home, and opened it. Of course, I should not have done it so early and unsurprisingly it registered negative. It was only October 9th and another four days till I took the test for real. Seeing that single pink line and *Not Pregnant* made me suspect that it would probably be confirmed negative on Saturday too. There was nothing I could do to change anything, but I just wanted to prepare myself for a sad result.

Eventually on October 12th, after a long sleepless night, I announced to David I was going to do the test. I needed him to be there for support.

"Before I do this, David, let me just ask you one thing. If it is a *Not Pregnant*, will you be prepared to carry on, maybe using a donor egg? I can't do this knowing a negative result will be the end of the road."

When he said yes, I was comforted.

Locking myself in the bathroom, I dreaded what the outcome was going to be. One pink stick, and one blue stick just to make certain, and a *Not Pregnant* as clear as day on both sticks. I had prepared as best as I possibly could for a negative answer but was still overcome by the wave of sadness, disappointment, and distress which stayed with me for the rest of the day.

We were back to square one.

Despite all the reiki, my therapy, and keeping fit and healthy, nothing had made any difference and Sam's final egg and all that hope dissolved into nothingness. My womb remained as empty as my heart, and I longed so much for a cuddle with Rosie.

Somehow that evening, I managed to put on some make-up, dress up, and go with Ellie to support Ella's fundraising evening. The world still turned, and we had to go through the motions. Helene needed our support as Ella's condition became more difficult, and it was a relief to think about someone else.

The Logan Centre
October 2006

David agreed we could look for another hospital willing to treat an older couple. However, this meant repeating all the counselling at a new hospital, having to explain about Rosie again, and regurgitating all the painful memories. It would mean a long wait for a donor egg to become available. Was this even feasible at my age? I was almost fifty-two years old. With all the expense, stress, time, and nervous energy, there was no guarantee of success. There would be more heartache and disappointment with failure. But I wasn't ready to give up, so there was no alternative.

During one of my long conversations with Val, she had mentioned an IVF specialist who she had heard treated women over fifty. I spent hours surfing the internet and found a news story about Professor Ian Craft, who treated older women at the Logan Centre for Assisted Reproduction in London. I emailed him and asked him if he would take on someone who was over fifty, how long was his waiting list for donor eggs, and could we please have an appointment?

The Logan Centre responded by return advising that they treated ladies up to the age of fifty-five and that the waiting time in the UK was about three years, but they also had an overseas programme in Cyprus where the waiting time was about six months.

They treated women up to age fifty-five! However, I was alarmed to learn the length of waiting time in the UK and that they required a substantial deposit. The estimated full treatment cost ran into thousands of pounds and even more if we went to Cyprus for treatment in their centre, although the waiting list there was only six months. All my previous treatment had been a lot cheaper, presumably because we already had Sam's donor eggs. The Logan Centre also expected you to advertise for a donor at additional cost. They would place the advert and add the fee to my account.

Joining an endless three-year waiting list for UK treatment was probably not ideal since I would be fifty-four years old by the time an egg hatched for me, so it may have to be Cyprus or nothing. Anyway, what was wrong with Cyprus? We were only six months and a four-and-a-half-hour flight away from the possibility rather than a long three-year wait. My heart skipped a beat when I read it. It stipulated that it is not essential for the man to go over there. David's sperm could be frozen here and sent by air courier to Limassol, where it could be kept in the deep freeze until I was ready.

When David came home from work and was given the update about the Logan Centre's treatment options and likely cost, he said that provided I could raise the funds, we could go ahead.

Exploring Adoption
November 2006

Strangely David started to chuck thoughts about adoption in my direction. I was very shocked since till now he had been adamantly against it. He also mentioned surrogacy, but women over fifty would not qualify. I started to research adoption, spending hours looking up which countries would allow us to adopt at our age. I came across a website called *Rainbow Adoptions*. It could be a sign, I joked to myself. Children of every nationality on there all desperate for a mummy and daddy. We could have one from each country in every bedroom. I knew there were all sorts of pitfalls, but it was a consideration. The thought of offering family and education to a child from abroad was growing on me. Just imagine our house filled with Chinese orphans.

I called the Royal Borough of Windsor and Maidenhead adoption services. A woman in their offices provided me with some information, which was an introduction to the leaflets and information she said she would send me. It choked me to even make the call on such a painful subject. The dreaded question came, of course, the voice down the line asking, "Do you have children?" So, I retold Rosie's story for the zillionth time.

Then she warned me that during the intensive investigations into our lives and histories, we would inevitably be asked whether we felt that our adopted child would be a replacement for Rosie. We could be offered a child round the ages of eight to ten years. I tried to visualise how that could be. On one hand the positives would bring us noise and activity and someone to cuddle, whom we could offer a chance in life. On the negative side could we handle any serious issues an adopted child might bring through no fault of their own?

So, we decided not to pursue adoption. I started saving up for a new course of treatment at the Logan Centre using a donor egg. This was going to take some time, so I threw myself into my work, grateful for the support of my dearest friends.

Our Third Attempt at IVF
November 2007

Through 2007 the school and charity were busy. We ran a successful Rosie's Rainbow retreat in a lovely old manor house in Devon for parents with severely disabled children. A group of mums who desperately needed the respite and a pamper enjoyed an escape with healing therapies, fluffy dressing gowns, delicious food, and fresh windy coastal walks.

Now back from the retreat, I was ready to pursue another option. For the whole of 2007, I had been saving hard for another shot at IVF. It had taken a year to accumulate funds, so following my fifty-third birthday, I booked an appointment for late November at the Logan Centre clinic.

The Victorian building was impressive and attractive. There was a comfortable sofa in the waiting room and a pretty cornice round the high ceiling, glossy magazines, and piles of leaflets were on the table. I flicked through a *Country Life* magazine, feeling a slight pang of guilt since back at school we had so much to organise due to an unexpected Ofsted inspection and an inspector expecting reams of paperwork and policies on her desk by nine the next morning. So, this was taking up my headspace on the train to Paddington. I was certainly not in baby mode and in the back of my mind was thinking that perhaps this wasn't such a good idea after all.

But then I met the Dutch doctor Cecille De Graaf. She didn't think I was crazy at all. Instead, she gave me confidence that this could work. A 30–40% chance of pregnancy and the knowledge that many older women were coming through these days and achieving significant success. This became even more encouraging when she gave me information about the new IVF clinic just opened in Alicante, Spain. Since it had recently opened, this clinic had no waiting list. It seemed a sensible choice, although I had to get my head around who the egg donor might be. The clinic matched your physical characteristics, and you had a choice of whether to accept or refuse the donor they identified as a possible match.

In Spain they would test for hepatitis, AIDS, HIV, etc. and it seemed safe enough. So, after a consultation, blood tests, and an ultrasound scan, I was advised everything looked good to go. The next step would be for David to go for his blood tests and to see the counsellor there. It all seemed familiar, and despite my history of failed cycles, I felt very different in this place.

Choosing my moment to prepare David for his part was crucial. A week later when we woke up, in my most casual tone, I mentioned the fact that next morning we had to be at the Logan Centre clinic by 9am. Suddenly he sprang out of bed and shot off towards the stairs. "What are you doing?" I called to him as he vanished through the bedroom door. "Going downstairs," he muttered. And for the rest of the day, it was just as though the shutters had come down. I was completely unnerved but decided not to press the point and hoped that he would be okay to keep our appointment.

I didn't sleep well that night, awake every hour till 5am, at which point I had woken David by mistake, so he went downstairs and stayed there for the rest of the night in front of the TV.

I lay sleepless for another hour. When I went downstairs his body language told me all was not well!

"I am not going. I don't want to do this."

I felt so panicked. "David, you can't go back on your word now. You agreed a few weeks ago."

"You are too old, I am too old. I just don't want this," David said.

It was only 6.15 and still dark, but I slipped Alfie's lead on and took him out for a walk, trying to breathe and regain composure, praying that David would change his mind and get dressed. When I returned an hour later, he was dressed and ready, although you could cut the air with a knife. The taxi pulled up outside our door and we caught the train to London. The carriage to Paddington was packed full of commuters and we hardly talked all the way there. I was trying to hold it together so that we could get through the counselling session without me breaking down into a blubbering wreck. Arriving in Devonshire Street, we managed a coffee at the nearby Boulangerie. I hoped that David had just had a bit of a wobble this morning and that everything would be okay.

The counsellor was kind and patient. Not surprisingly she immediately picked up on David's body language. She could see he was feeling uncomfortable, and he clearly wanted to be anywhere else on earth rather than sitting opposite a counsellor. We had to go through the whole Rosie tragedy, which was so difficult for us both. She asked how we dealt with our grief for Rosie. I explained about the charity, David's obsession with the gym, and that somehow we coped with it despite our differences.

The counsellor then asked how I felt at that moment, and I had to be honest and tell her that I was choking back tears. We discussed all the implications of having IVF treatment. To my enormous relief David was cooperative. We were told that at this clinic the recent success rate was almost 50%.

"How would we feel if they were twins?" she asked. I said gobsmacked but delighted, of course. Even David said, "Fantastic. We had twins in our families." Had we talked to Ellie and my family? Had we considered my physical age, and could we cope both emotionally and physically? So many questions and so many issues, but it was apparent to her that we had thought it all through and were not walking blindly into it.

Then there was the first mention of having the treatment in Cyprus instead of Spain, which was explained more fully to us. It all seemed very well planned, and I didn't feel too worried about having to travel there. The waiting list was about six months. Most of the egg donors in the Cyprus clinic were not Cypriot but were women from Eastern Bloc countries, Russia, Moldova, or Ukraine. This was a complete revelation, but I didn't experience any concern over that either. My family claimed some Russian heritage, and I understood that many

Russians were artistic, passionate, creative, and musical. The counsellor wished us well said she hoped it worked for us. David and I had to fill in forms stating our own physical characteristics and what characteristics we would look for in an egg donor. I found this part a bit like filling in an online Tesco shopping order and choosing what apples and brand of washing powder you want delivered.

With the meeting over I accompanied David down the road to have his blood tests and since we didn't have to wait long and the woman taking his blood was very gentle, David came away smiling, saying, "Well, since we are going to do this, and we are going to try and make a baby and there is no going back, then I think you need my support as it's a big thing really!"

We went home to wait.

To Share or Not to Share
February 2008

Christmas came and went and in February I sent an email to the Logan Centre clinic to enquire whether we were any nearer the top of the list. They responded straight away saying they would keep us informed.

That day I drove to High Wycombe to see a medium called Valerie, who I had heard about through the Maidenhead Spiritualist Church.

Arriving at her little lemon-coloured bungalow, she showed me into the room where she conducted her readings. It was an ordinary kind of dining room, but the shelves were filled with pictures of White Eagle and other spiritual-looking ornaments. She said that she would try to link with my daughter but couldn't promise. I hadn't even told her I had a girl but had said I wanted to link with my child. She didn't know my surname or anything about me. I had never met her before, yet she somehow seemed to know. The first thing she said was that my daughter was surrounded by colour and that she loved colour and was showing me rainbows. I knew it was Rosie. She described her chirpy, busy personality. She said she was most certainly with Tessie her dog and that she was beside me too and urging me to carry on with all I was doing. She described how she was in the light and surrounded by colour and flowers and was happy. It all sounds clichéd, but I believed that she was being totally upfront with me and came across as being a sincere and compassionate lady. She then asked for a photo, which I showed her. It was one of Ellie and Rosie cuddling Tessie. She enquired whether I'd lost a baby as she saw Rosie holding a baby. I said no, I had not, and she went on to say that she felt this baby was either one who was in spirit or one who was about to come to earth, and did I know anyone who was about to have a birth? I said I did but not in the family!

I confided then that I was about to undergo IVF and was it possible that this baby Rosie was holding could be the same one? Valerie said she didn't know; she could only say what she had already said, that there was a baby coming, and that was all.

She gave me much-needed validation when she said, "You know Rosie really is with you in everything you do, and I can hear her telling you, *Mum, I really don't need a medium to tell you all this; I am telling you myself. I'm right here.*"

When Valerie had finished, I produced a Rosie's Rainbow leaflet and gave it to her. She was astounded and visibly moved.

"Well, there you are, you see; you are doing such positive things. Where you could have turned your grief in on yourself, you chose to do something wonderful in your daughter's memory. While it is so awfully sad you lost your child and there is nothing which will take this pain away, isn't it incredible that so much good is coming from it and so many children are benefitting? I firmly believe that people come into this life knowing that they are only here for so long. Souls decide before they arrive and no matter how much you wonder why she was taken so soon, she chose to leave when she did. Her work was done, she had achieved what she came for, and nothing anyone can do could change that. I feel it's almost as if your roles have reversed and that although she was your child, she is telling me you are almost her child, and she is guiding you and looking after and protecting you."

I cried all the way home, feeling drained but also happy that Rosie was with me.

On my arrival home there was an email from the Logan Centre clinic with an offer of an egg donor. This took me by surprise as I had thought it would be several months till we would hear anything. A spreadsheet was attached with physical details, blood group, and a little about the donor. The match wasn't perfect, but it was an option. I was also offered this egg as an 'exclusive donation'. If you are offered a donor whose eggs are only given to one recipient, it is much more expensive than if you share a donor egg cycle with another person.

I received a further email from the clinic assuming we were probably going to accept the 'exclusive donation', requesting an upfront payment of £11,500. Although I was expecting it to be expensive, it was a lot more than I bargained for. How could I afford this sum of money which did not even cover flights to Cyprus, accommodation, or even medication? The clinic needed a decision in three days' time.

The next few days were exhausting as I was spending all my waking hours trying to weigh up the pros and cons. Whichever way I looked at it, I just did not have the funds to pay for an 'exclusive donation'. So, I wrote to the clinic asking them to place me back on the waiting list until they found a donor who was willing to do a 'shared cycle'. In the meantime, I would have to wait for that opportunity to happen. I was truly fed up and frustrated with the whole process.

It was a beautiful sunny day, and I was out walking Alfie. It was unusual for a February day to be so warm, with a clear azure sky and all the birds being particularly vocal. A family were out on a Saturday afternoon bike ride. There was the mum, a dad, and two little girls. They were just a normal family doing normal stuff together. I should have felt pleased they were enjoying themselves on such a bright spring day, but all that washed over me was a painful memory.

I explained to Sam that I had been put back on the waiting list for an egg share, which would halve the bill. Sam was worried about the effects of yet more shattered hope. She was concerned that if this went wrong, I wouldn't have the mental ability to cope with it these days and she didn't want to watch the three of us go through more pain.

A Donor from Moldova
March 2008

On February 26th, a possible recipient was identified who would be willing to do a shared cycle.

I had less than twenty-four hours to decide. David went into one of his silent moods, leaving me struggling alone to make the decision.

Ellie was out for most of the weekend. At nearly twenty years of age, she was almost independent. I spent hours walking the dog and thinking and then overthinking and by evening was feeling quite wretched and confused. Rereading the donor details over and over, I wondered about this lady from Moldova. Why was she offering her eggs? What was her current child like? Could this woman who I would probably never meet be the one to change my world? My imagination was running away with me – again!

For better or worse I had to go ahead.

After much persuasion David agreed to accompany me to Cyprus for one last try!

On Thursday, February 28th, 2008, I emailed the clinic with my answer. The clinic would be sending all the relevant documents. Val was the only person who understood and was totally supportive. "You will never forgive yourself if in your dotage you sit there thinking, well, it could have been but that you never gave it your final try. It's brilliant, how exciting. I look at our three beautiful little boys in their cots and know we were right when we did it, so you need to do this."

We would be flying to Cyprus at the end of March or beginning of April. I was scared, but at least this time I was going in with my eyes wide open and knew I could cope with a negative outcome. I decided not to tell Mum yet but would at least have to discuss this with Ellie.

One week later on March 7th, I set off for the Logan Centre. This was absolutely my last chance saloon. This time round, there was more than just myself to consider. There was also the egg donor in Moldova.

This was different from the first and second time around and I didn't experience any gut feeling about this at all. I saw all the pain ahead if it didn't work, and the worry if it did! Would it possible to bond with the egg of a Moldovan woman who I would never meet and who did not even speak my language? If this worked, would I feel that this child was really all mine, or would I have a problem bonding because it would not have mine or my family's genes? What if I didn't bond with him/her and feel like a mother at all? I was so afraid and yet still wanted this so very much.

My apprehension about telling Ellie was forestalled when she rang me to say she was coming home. I warned her I wouldn't be around as I was in London. We arranged to meet at Paddington so we could travel home together. As soon as we met, she asked, "What are you doing in London then?"

"I'm just having one last bash at the IVF thing." I put on my brightest, most confident voice which I hoped would mask the nervous wreck lying just beneath the flippant surface. She gave me a disapproving sideways glance and her answer was immediate.

"Get real. It's not going to happen. You are too OLD. How old are you?" She looked at me as though I had lost the plot. "Mum, let's book a holiday."

"We will do, but not right now."

"I really want to go to Dubai. Let's go to Dubai."

I grabbed the cue. "Well, Ellie, we could have a couple of days in Cyprus?"

I explained that the treatment would be happening there as it cut down the waiting time from two years to three months. "No, I really only want to go to Dubai!" She sighed. It was not quite the response I needed, but I was relieved that she hadn't thrown a total tantrum. She was a lot older now, of course. She rapidly steered the conversation towards our upcoming plans for the latest Rosie's Rainbow Fund charity gala we were staging at the Wycombe Swan Theatre the following month. I was more than happy to change the subject to the safe territory of theatre talk, chatting about casting the show and her bunch of college buddies who were coming to perform. I was careful not to mention Cyprus again that day.

Over the next week my feet didn't touch the ground. There was so much to do to prepare for the gala. It was to be a big event in the thousand-seat theatre in High Wycombe. I was chuffed and proud that so many West End artistes and professionals had committed to giving their time and talents to raise money in Rosie's honour. Adam was producer again, and we spent time together brainstorming this production which would be our most ambitious to date. He was fabulous company, a friend who always lifted my spirits and made me laugh. As a long-time serving patron of the charity, he pulled all the stops out, enlisting his West End mates to come and perform. My line-up included Jayne. I had shared everything baby-related with her over the years from our trips to New York and Paris until now and had to find some time to bring her up to date. Our cast list included stars from *Phantom of the Opera*, *Billy Elliot*, *We will Rock You*, an Elvis tribute band, and 250 excited performers from Redroofs. Crucial meetings took place with Adam to sort the production schedule, running order, and lighting and sound requirements for the show. There were trips to the Wycombe Swan to plan dressing room allocations, and Rosie's Rainbow Fund meetings with Helene Bev and Candice to sort raffle prizes, front of house, catering to keep our artistes fed and watered on the day, and thank you gifts to source for the artistes, plus children's rehearsals, chaperones, and costume fittings to schedule. Lucy Benjamin was invited to draw the raffle. It was certainly a lot to deal with when I was preparing myself both physically and mentally for a very different sort of production.

During that week I squeezed in a Logan Centre trip, where they had now started my treatment in readiness for transfer in a few weeks. Alongside this, David was making his trip to the clinic, ready to give his sperm – his own performance! Apart from stating concern about getting lost on the underground, he was very calm, and if I hadn't known the many doubts we had about it in the past, I would have said he appeared to be almost looking forward to it!

I arrived at the clinic early morning for an injection which made me feel really weird. The nurse had jabbed the mega long needle into my thigh, and for the rest of the day, it made me very sore and achy. It felt as though she had rammed it right into my bone and I felt sick and queasy.

By lunchtime I was back in our studio, sitting through an afternoon of end of term plays and was informed by David when I called him at the end of the afternoon that he had done well, too. I had a text from Ellie saying, *I just want u to know I've been thinking and want u to know I'm ok with this whole IVF thing I will support you all the way.* My oldest daughter was growing up and I was touched and thankful that she was so accepting this time around.

On the way to walk Alfie next morning, I drove past our old house. I saw a ladder in the window of our old bedroom, and they were painting the room. I couldn't help looking. We had painted that room in a soft lilac. The lilac had now gone. I had a photo of Rosie in the room taken on her eleventh birthday. In that photo she was posing on my bed. She was wearing her pink hat, her stripy over-the-knee socks, her long legs drawn up to her chest, and she was wearing a little blue denim skirt and a new pink long-sleeve top with the butterfly on the front. She was not too well when we took the pictures, her weight had dropped, she had a cough and dark shadows under her eyes. Her face was paler than usual, but I clearly remembered photographing her on December 17th, 2002.

I wondered what colour they had painted the walls now and whether Rosie ever 'visited' her old house.

I was visiting the clinic almost daily for scans and one day great big black circles on the screen revealed an ovarian cyst. The nurse reassuringly pointed out that these cysts were commonplace and spring up from seemingly nowhere then disappear as quickly. However, if it didn't go away in a week, I would have to go in and have it aspirated, which sounded horrible! The treatment couldn't continue until the cyst had gone, so I was left in limbo for a few days. Was I barking mad? Why in the hell was I putting myself through all of this? Amanda, our Rosie's Rainbow therapist, gave me a timely aromatherapy massage at her home. Since I was undergoing treatment, I needed to enlighten Amanda about the plans, particularly as different oils react with pregnancy and conception etc. The massage left me spaced out, but Amanda cooked homemade leek soup and we chatted for a while about Rosie and how I coped, which released a lot of tears. It felt awkward to be sobbing uncontrollably into the soup, but Amanda seemed okay with it and simply said I needed to cry. This was true, as I was still rarely able to find real tears, but after that I spent the rest of the day sitting on the sofa watching TV and feeling ghastly.

Over the next week, to my relief, the cyst shrank! The scan showed it had decreased from five centimetres to just one and was disappearing of its own volition, so I started taking Progynova twice a day. The clinic said I should be in Cyprus within two and a half to three weeks. None of this felt real and I was now on the course of tablets synchronised with both the Moldovan guitar-playing veterinary surgeon egg donor and the anonymous lady who was sharing the eggs with me.

The long-awaited letter from the London Fertility Centre arrived, informing me the eggs were being collected from the Moldovan donor on April 17th. There were details about my medication and the careful timing of tablets in the run up to the day, and instructions to be in Cyprus for my embryo transfer on the morning of Tuesday, April 22nd, 2008.

Cyprus
April 2008

We were due to fly to Cyprus on Monday morning! The Moldovan donor's eggs were ready to be harvested in just one day's time, so once the egg entered the test tube and David's frozen sperm had been mixed, our embryo would be in the wings and ready to make an entrance. The embryo transfer was happening on Tuesday morning in Limassol. Our flights were booked from Heathrow and reservations made at a hotel.

Ellie was totally fine with it this time and was all smiles when I told her it was imminent.

I phoned Mum. "Hi, just to let you know that next week David and I are going to have a few days away, er, in, um… Cyprus." I expected her to ask what I was thinking of going abroad on the first day of term, with a huge show coming up in a few weeks. But she said, "What a good idea!"

Adam and I visited the Wycombe Swan on Friday morning for a technical meeting and to look at the stage in preparation for the gala. We had a pleasant lunch, courtesy of Adam, and laughed a lot! As he chatted about lighting and production ideas, I realised that one week from then I would either be pregnant, or not. I tried not to think any more about it and to pay attention to my cast lists.

I was changing some pounds for euros in NatWest when it hit me, and I thought Jesus Christ, this is really happening. My stomach was doing cartwheels.

I was on the home run and the preparation for transfer was almost complete.

Sam presented me with half a dozen newly laid eggs from her chickens and a note handwritten by Sasha which read *fresh laid eggs for your collection!*

Amanda treated me to another aromatherapy massage on Sunday. It was so good being pampered and I left very chilled with her good wishes and positive vibes.

On Monday, April 21st, 2008, we flew to Cyprus for our final attempt. I was tense, unsure whether my nerves were due to the flying or the situation. I had bought a bottle of Bach Rescue Remedy and knocked it back as if it was going out of fashion. At the other end a taxi drove us to Limassol, arriving to glorious weather. We checked into the hotel. As we entered the hotel lobby, there was a massive colourful Easter egg decoration centre stage. It transpired we had arrived over the Cypriot Easter holiday and the place was looking festive. It was as though the egg had been placed there specially to greet us. Up in the hotel room, I put too much bath foam in the Jacuzzi and the whole thing frothed up till I felt like I was drowning in whipped-up egg whites. I laughed out loud. David was flaked out on the bed and said he was too tired to come and see, but I think Rosie would have been amused. Sitting on the comfy chair on the hotel balcony wrapped in a fluffy white hotel bathrobe and slippers, I closed my eyes and tried to relax and savour this surreal moment in the balmy Cypriot evening sun. We dressed and went down for dinner, where we indulged in a wonderful Chinese meal and hoped we would be able to make the most of the hotel facilities for the next few days. We must have been the only couple in the hotel who were not there for a holiday. I wished Ellie had been with us too. We really were on the strangest adventure.

I tossed and turned most of the night. Awake at 3am and unable to get back to sleep, I read for an hour then drifted into one of those disturbed sleeps where images and dreams seem so real. I dreamed I had been given a baby to look after. He had a mop of red curly hair, and I felt no attachment or connection to him. I was trying to find his mother to give him back but was unable to find her. In my dream I was thinking, oh no, this baby is staying, and I don't even like him!

David woke me at 7am and I felt tired and headachy. Being too nervous to eat, breakfast was a waste of time. Forcing down the requisite three glasses of liquid, I wondered how I was going to cope with a very full bladder.

We ordered a taxi. "Ah, Limassol Clinic. The best one," said the taxi driver as we left the hotel. David pointed out two colossal baskets containing bright red Easter eggs. They must have been seven feet wide and took up the whole centre of the coast road as we were driven towards the clinic. Bizarrely there were eggs literally everywhere. We passed a nightclub called Rosy's Bar. I wondered whether she knew.

The Genesis Clinic Limassol was a white building located in a side road. Arriving at 8.45am sharp we made our way upstairs. Never having set foot in a Cypriot clinic, I was a bag of nerves, but the clinic was pristine, and the staff friendly and courteous. I was taken down a corridor past a row of very pink frilly cribs where tiny new-born babies were making little noises. With some surprise I realised it was a maternity ward too and that people gave birth here.

The treatment room was white and clean. There was a bed with stirrups and an oddly shaped front which resembled a toilet bowl. The room contained several machines, a scanner, and lots of baby pictures on the walls. "Please get yourself ready and climb on the bed," said the nurse.

"Relax and don't be nervous. So many girls lie on this bed, and believe me, they return in nine months to have their babies here!"

Enter Dr Zavvos Khoundouros. He was an attractive man in his late thirties with dark kind eyes and a friendly manner. He said gently, "Now, Carolyn, I would like to have a little chat. Why do you look so nervous?"

I heard myself laugh and reply, "I'm not nervous; I just need the loo!"

"Okay, okay," he said, smiling. "Then let's get on with it and we will talk after that. But I must tell you, you had six embryos of which three fertilised and here we have two truly excellent ones."

The nurse pressed the scanner thing on my stomach as he studied the image of my uterus on the monitor. "Your endometrial lining is beautiful and the thickness, it is eleven." I felt proud that he had admired my *beautiful* lining. "This will work!" he said. After that we seemed to wait for ages, although it probably wasn't more than five minutes, and then another doctor entered the room to assist him.

At last, the syringe arrived bearing the two embryos and he popped them straight in. It was quick and painless and then it was over. I was told to lie and relax, and Dr Zavvos said again, "This will work. What did they tell you about your endometrium in London?"

"Uh, nothing much."

"Well, let me tell you, Carolyn, it is perfect and beautiful, and your embryos are excellent."

"You sound very sure," I said.

"Yes, yes, I am sure everything is perfect for us to have a pregnancy."

"At my age? I am fifty-three, you know."

"Fifty-three? I do this on sixty-three! I don't like to do this on sixty-three, but I do, so fifty-three, it is nothing, absolutely nothing. It is all good. You have a good chance here." That was it. I was besotted. "Now, I have put in two embryos, and I have frozen one embryo. Maybe you will have twins, but one will be better, easier to cope with. You keep taking the medication and do a pregnancy test a week on Saturday." I dressed and crossed my legs while he shook David's hand and explained to him all he had told me, then thankfully I dashed for the loo.

I asked David to take a photo outside the clinic before we caught a taxi back to the hotel. The rest of the day was spent by the pool in the hot sunshine. It was very civilised, and I felt so lucky. I tried to chill out and process the day's events. David didn't want to discuss it. He said he needed a stiff whisky and that he felt he was living someone else's life.

Leaving David relaxing by the pool, I went to check out the beach. Sitting on the rocks paddling my feet in the warm blue sea, I texted Helene, Amanda and Val, then called Sam. On my mobile I relayed the entire experience. Then I returned to the pool and my sunbed and lay with my legs propped right up, almost like an upside down fruit bat.

The next evening, we dined at a restaurant across the road from the hotel. Spending time with David was unusual these days. We found plenty to talk about. I was chatting away ten to the dozen about the egg donor and trying to work out where on the atlas Moldova was, and said it was definitely Eastern Bloc, somewhere near Russia, and what a generous, utterly amazing thing this Moldavan lady had done. His reaction was bizarre. It was as if I had dropped a monumental bombshell.

His knife and fork slipped out of his hands, and he spat out a chunk of steak. "Russian? What do you mean Russian?" I was staggered that despite having shown him the donor details several times, he clearly hadn't taken in what was written down.

"I told you she was Moldovan."

"You did not."

"I DID!"

"I told my brothers it was a Greek egg."

"David, I cannot believe you have not processed this potentially life-changing information. I am literally staggered that we have managed to get this far, and we are sitting here in Cyprus, and you didn't know where the egg you have inseminated is coming from."

I sat stunned while he took a large gulp of beer. All I could think to say to him was "Well, you can UN-tell them." The truth was, of course, that David had switched off and his answers and remarks over the past weeks were mostly "whatever", "you sort it", "yeah yeah yeah okay". He really hadn't processed the crucial facts.

Next morning before we went down to breakfast, he stood peering out of the bedroom window onto the Limassol Street below. Then he turned to me and half to me but half to himself, he exclaimed, "Jesus Christ, I've fertilised a frigging Russian!" Then he went off for a massage and I was left for a couple of hours to lie by the pool in glorious sunshine, sipping ice-cold sparkling water, thinking by this time next year our lives may have changed so much, or if the test is negative, then I will be free to do so much. To take holidays, travel, run the charity, grow the business. If I have this child, I will have to change so many things, curtail all these activities, not go abroad with Ellie and yet the joy and possible fulfilment of mothering another child, a baby boy (because I did feel it would be a boy) would far outweigh any of the other stuff.

The following evening over dinner, we talked again of the possibility that perhaps, just perhaps, this IVF treatment had done its magic. I asked David, "So, is it just possible that you want this pregnancy to happen?" He shrugged.

"Well, I guess some part of me must want it or I wouldn't have come." If nothing else, the break was good for David. Working seven days a week to keep his grief and sadness at bay had worn him out and it was good to see him more relaxed.

Downstairs in the piano bar we found a seat in a quiet corner. It was our final evening, so we thought we might as well make the best of it. We ordered drinks in the attractive darkened lounge. It was peaceful in there and a pianist was playing a large white grand piano. Hearing music, I once again experienced that acute and familiar stab of sadness. As it washed over me, tears started to drip down my face and there was nothing I could do to stop them. I used up all the serviettes which were on the table and the waitress who saw me weeping buckets quickly replaced them with another bundle. "I think the waitress saw you needed them," whispered David as I snivelled and blew. "I'm just having a moment. I'll be okay in a minute." I gulped. As I said that the pianist started playing 'Somewhere Over the Rainbow' and water just poured out of my eyes. David also looked grief-stricken. Here were Rosie's mummy and daddy on holiday but no Rosie – well, not in the flesh anyway.

All week we had been observing parents playing with and cuddling their little ones, messing about in the pool with their kids with not a care in the world, and I guess it was understandable that it suddenly overwhelmed us both. I doubted it would ever change. However, we had arrived as a pair and could be returning to England as a three. At that moment it seemed the most impossible thing in the world.

Rosie's Rainbow Gala
April 2008

The week after arriving home, I felt intermittently nauseous and headachy, but thought it could be a bug because David hadn't been feeling great either. Every five minutes I examined my body for changes despite being heavily bogged down with the Rosie's Rainbow Gala. The show was only a week and a bit away and things were getting tense, so I didn't know whether the feeling was stress because of the show or... could it be? It was undoubtedly odd, but I didn't feel like myself at all. I only had two more days to wait, but I dreaded seeing a negative on the stick. It was just a week and three days until Rosie's Rainbow charity show, *Starry Starry Night*, and there was so much still to be done. I must have been bonkers to have agreed to staging such a huge show.

Pregnant
May 2008

Dr Zavvos said to do a pregnancy test on May 3rd. That was today! Waiting till David arrived home, I tried to prepare myself for a result either way, but it was more difficult than I thought. I did feel queasy, but Sam suggested it was the medication, which was more likely since I was still stuffing myself with hormones.

David arrived home at 6pm, immediately went to the fridge, and filled a plate with cold chicken drumsticks and some salad. He disappeared into the living room and switched on the telly. He hadn't noticed the unopened test which had been sitting on the kitchen sideboard. All day long I had been staring at the packet. I picked it up, locked myself in the loo, and did the test. My hand was shaking as I placed it on the kitchen table and sat there, stomach churning, staring at the little window on the blue test stick. David was watching a very obscure war film on TV. The word *PREGNANT* just popped up as clear as anything. I heard myself just repeating, "Oh my God, oh my God, oh my God" and showed David the stick. "I'm pregnant! Oh my God."

David initially displayed no reaction whatsoever and continued to watch the television. But after a few minutes, he started to absorb the news.

I wanted to break the news to Ellie, but she had gone to a birthday party in Leeds and would not be home till Monday, so I would have to be patient until then.

I tried to call Sam, but she texted that she was in the pictures and kept asking what I wanted. While I was waiting for her to call me back, I texted Val, *Oh my God, I'm pregnant.* She called me straight away, saying, "Oh my God, oh my God, oh my God, I need a cigarette."

David was very quiet, then paced around the house before saying, "You won't forget Rosie, will you?" I couldn't believe he thought that I could ever forget our beautiful daughter.

"I believe she has organised it. David, I've said it before, she is responsible for this," I replied. He had arranged to go out for a drink with Mike, Helene's husband. Helene had offered to be chauffeur and drive him over. Summoning her into my hall and unable to contain myself, I announced my pregnancy. She screamed and threw her arms round me. I felt so many things, euphoric, happy, stunned, but mostly overwhelmed.

I called Val again as I walked Alfie round the common. She said, "This is the single most wonderful gift that Rosie could give you. This is so life-affirming, and it is totally not about forgetting Rosie."

She continued, "But your world will be turned upside down." Yes, I thought, it would certainly do that. But perhaps we would experience some joy. Ellie would have a sibling here on earth where she could physically hold him/her, hug him/her, feel him/her, and see him/her. Rosie was sending us this life-changing gift and, all being well, I wanted to savour every single moment. Mum took it all in and wished us "Mazel tov." It was good to share the news with her and she seemed very happy if slightly conflicted. I was aware that this was a difficult thing for her to process and hoped she would be happy for us. I even repeated the test which again confirmed *Pregnant*, still unable to process it or imagine that in eight months I would be carrying a baby around. I emailed the Logan Centre to share the good news.

I didn't find the right moment to break the news to Ellie until she was back from London two days later. She startled me by saying, "Mum, I already know. You left an email open, the one to the clinic." She said she was very shocked and didn't know how she felt about the news. "Mum, I am worried about you. You are just so old!" I tried to say the right thing, but as usual nothing right came out. I felt stupid.

Later she texted five times to say:

1. Love you too. Sorry I was shocked it really is such a big shock.

2. I just need time to think things through. It a really big shock, mum

3. Love you

4. I love you

5. I love you

I texted back that I loved her too.

The Show Goes On
May 2008

Plans were coming together for the weekend show at the Wycombe Swan. I was engrossed in organising the big event when I noticed a small bleed. In a panic, I called the clinic and spoke to a nurse. She instructed me to increase the Cyclogest and rest up over the weekend. I increased the medication and realised I would have to try to be sensible on the day of the show and let everyone else do the running about. I had to stop, lie down, and most importantly calm down, which was not something I was good at, especially when it was an important and exciting gala event for Rosie. Adam was a gem and had pulled out all the stops to help with the production. He had the help of a West End stage manager and sound engineer, which gave me peace of mind that the technical part should run smoothly. We sold 1,076 tickets and had a list waiting for returns.

As our charity benefitted local children, we were pleased to have received a grant from Wycombe Council to help towards costs. It was all looking promising for raising a good sum for Rosie's Rainbow. Our hallway was piled up with banners, tea urns, theatre programmes, bags, packs of crisps, bottles of water, and all manner of stuff ready to be transported.

It was a real family affair. Ellie was on her way home from spending the night out with her college friends. She was excited to be performing in the show and we had booked a coach to transport twenty of her dance student friends who were taking part. Rowan and Sasha were to sing in the ensemble. Sam was taking photos. Ludo and Fiona were travelling from Stratford and Robin and all of Rosie's cousins would be coming to see the show. In my head I asked Rosie to make the show a success and to please keep an eye on me under the circumstances!

The big day arrived and as we unloaded backstage it felt full of promise. The sun was already shining and hot although it was early in the day. Adam was there getting the resident crew sorted and the

Steinway piano was tuned and placed stage right, waiting for our accompanist. It felt rather like a wedding when, after months of planning, you are so caught up in the whirlwind that you cannot appreciate the moment and it all flies by too fast. It was wonderful to greet all our West End cast as they arrived for their soundchecks. I was surrounded by the buzz and chaos of the day and trying to organise 250 very excited but hot kids who had arrived ready dressed in Rosie's show tee shirts in every colour of the rainbow and neat French plaits. David and his brothers were not going to miss out on another opportunity to perform. They had dined out for years on their original *Full Monty* performance and had rehearsed their own number which was going to provide the comic element. They had put in several weeks of evening rehearsals working on 'Hey Big Spender' with one of our lovely dance teachers. Up in the dressing rooms, bedecked in red sexy corsets bought from Ann Summers, fishnet tights, black Doc Marten boots, red feather boas, and assorted tarty wigs, they were now practising straddling their black chairs, hairy legs spread wide and suffering acute stage fright whilst awaiting their call to the stage for their rendition of 'Cell Block Tango' and 'Hey Big Spender'. Rosie's uncle Colin – David's brother – had, upon arrival, nervously entered stage left, walked to stage centre, taken one look at the thousand-seater auditorium and then to the top of the upper circle, and whispered in my ear, "Cor blimey. If I give you £1,000, can I go home now?" Many evenings had been spent practising and perfecting 'Pop, Six, Squish, Uh uh, Cicero, Lipschitz', so I just laughed and said there was no going back. I joined my showbiz friends Mazz and Gina. In their dressing room Mazz offered me a Bellini in a plastic stemmed glass. I just had a quick swig, not wishing to drink while I was pregnant. They were so supportive and happy to be there. A few years ago, I had taken Ellie and Rosie to see the musical version of *The Full Monty* which Gina was starring in at that time. My girls were besotted with the show and spent months singing all the songs and I had clear memories of Rosie in full throttle, belting out Gina's solo, "*He looks cute in a suit, and I love him to boot. I'm telling you, you gotta love that man.*" As patrons of Rosie's Rainbow Fund, Mazz and Gina were always ready to help even though they were both busy West End stars.

I shoved on some make-up, put on a dress, and headed back downstairs where the foyer was already filling with the audience. Family and friends had arrived and were trying to grab my attention. There were staff and nurses from John Radcliffe, including Christine the play specialist with whom Rosie had shared her wish to put on shows to raise money all those years ago. I did my best to chat to as many of the guests and audience as possible in between rushing about sorting last-minute issues before the curtain went up. I smiled so much my jaw was aching, and I was overheated, but I didn't care. I was so happy caught up in the magic of putting on a show for Rosie and knowing I was pregnant. In a corner of the foyer, I whispered the news to my brother Robin. He was quite overcome. A house seat was set aside for Lucy, who, as a patron of the charity, had come along to draw the raffle. In the interval I told her my news. She nearly fainted with excitement.

Adam Stafford and Joanne Froggatt draw the raffle

Jayne was in her dressing room, and I couldn't wait until the end of the show to tell her. She was so happy for us. It wasn't ideal timing, but I was swept up with the mood of the day and thought oh what the hell and what better place to tell exciting news than in a theatre! Adam did an extraordinary job. The show ran without a hitch and a great time was had by all. I think Rosie was very much there cheering us on, and we raised £13,000.

Scans
May 2008

Crashing down to earth with a bump after the adrenaline rush of the show, we dealt with the fifth anniversary of Rosie's passing on May 14th, a day I always dreaded. Angel days were always sad and this one seemed worse than ever, probably due to hormones and post-show blues.

Ellie took the day off from college, caught the train home, and came out for lunch with Bev, Candice, Helene, and Sam. With the company and support of our good friends, we got through the day.

As the week progressed, I started experiencing morning sickness and feeling extremely tired. My friends recommended ginger herbal tea and ginger biscuits, but they didn't really help much.

At the end of May, I booked our first scan. This was to see whether the pregnancy was viable and, if so, how many babies there were. I experienced mixed feelings of excitement and anxiety. What if there was no baby or if something was wrong?

In the scan room with the consultant Dr De Graaf was a woman who did all the pre-pregnancy scans and a lady who was in training. I lay on the couch with David behind just out of my view as Dr De Graaf slid the scanner into position. She turned the monitor round and said to us, "There is the baby, do you see?" I was witnessing a miracle as she pointed out the movement, a little rhythmic pulsating white blob in which I could detect a fluttering that was our baby's heartbeat. She confirmed there was one baby and it all looked very good indeed. As I dressed, she and the others were doing their calculations. My due date was January 10th, 2009.

It dawned on both of us that inside me there was a real living foetus and a new life. For me, it was a hopeful feeling, while David was perhaps still in shock. All the happenings of the last months were suddenly real when I saw that tiny heartbeat. She gave us a printout of the scan photo. David was silent. What was going on in his mind? With instructions to see my GP and start with the antenatal care, we left the clinic and walked down the road. David seemed to be in his own world.

He mumbled, "I just can't get my head around it. I can't help it."

Over the next few days, I made a concerted effort to back off and wait for David to get used to the reality.

I was already bonding with this new person growing inside me. And whilst I would always grieve and miss Rosie, I could not and would not ever let this child think he/she was second best.

On a shopping trip to Reading, I guiltily sneaked into the Mamas and Papas baby shop in the Oracle shopping centre. The cots, furniture, and buggies were so tempting as I admired some rather lovely nursery furniture and cute baby outfits. I had to almost drag myself out of there, my good sense saying it's too early, don't tempt fate, but my inner voice saying yes, but look how lovely they all are! It was not hard to imagine the baby's room, a space where David kept his gym equipment but would make a perfect nursery. It was the same room I had stood in all those years ago when all of this was just a pipe dream and I had daydreamed about Peter Rabbit accessories but never thought it would happen.

After two days of almost continuous silence between us, David finally brought up the subject. "I am just finding this so difficult. I can't get my head round it. Why did this have to happen to Rosie? Why, why, why? I feel that we have done so much since she went, and I feel so guilty. It's so weird starting over and it just doesn't feel the same."

"I don't know why, David, and we will never know why until we get to wherever Rosie is too. But surely a new life is better than no life and this new phase is at least hopeful. As long as this baby is healthy, how can it be a bad thing?"

I was even more surprised when he continued. "Do you want to find out what sex it is? I'd like it to be a girl, but you think it will be a boy, don't you?"

"David, I don't know what it is, although all those mediums have predicted a boy as far back as when we were in Cornwall and that medium woman who said that there would be a baby after a very long gap, but as long as it's healthy, then it doesn't matter."

I was thinking that the fact he had even expressed concern about the sex of the child was a good sign. So, I hoped that he would gradually get used to the idea and things would be okay. I was so tired of feeling bad all the time. Five years of pain and anguish was truly enough and while I knew I would never ever stop hurting and missing Rosie, we had to live a life and I didn't want to suffer anymore.

I went for an appointment with Dr Cathy Scothorne at Cookham surgery. She was the same doctor I had seen when the baby quest was just beginning. She was so pleased it had happened and was empathic and helpful. She didn't rush me and for twenty minutes we discussed the options. She made me feel safe and supported in the knowledge that she and Sally, the midwife who looked after all her pregnant ladies at Cookham surgery, would do the very best they could to help us achieve a positive outcome with understanding and consistency of care. She pointed out that we had to get through the next six weeks safely. There would be a scan for nuchal fold to detect Downs syndrome at twelve weeks and she advised me this birth was likely to be a Caesarean. This was my preferred option, mainly because I was so filled with dread at the prospect of going to Wexham Park Hospital, which held traumatic memories of Rosie's days there. Because of my age and the increased risk during pregnancy and birth, our health insurance company agreed they would cover the cost of private maternity care.

I was now eleven weeks pregnant and felt permanently knackered and sick. The queasiness was worse towards afternoon and evening, and I wondered why it was called morning sickness. Everything was progressing, and my waistline was expanding so much that I had already bought two pairs of maternity trousers. I now needed to keep calm and relaxed.

Following the excitement of the recent charity show, the summer term settled back into business as usual, with end of term dance exams and a general winding down towards the summer break. I was not sure whether my pupils had noticed my growing bump, but I didn't intend on sharing the news with them yet.

There were serious concerns about Helene's daughter Ella. She was in and out of hospital with increasing frequency. She was suffering from constant chest infections, and I was visiting when I could.

At twelve weeks, the morning sickness seemed to be diminishing. The scan for Downs syndrome was normal. I couldn't believe it went so well and the nurse reassured me everything looked fine. It was certainly very exciting to see baby rolling and twirling, the head, arms, feet, and body clearly visible and looking exactly as they should. I kept worrying that something bad would happen. Having seen so much tragedy, so many families with handicapped children, I felt it was almost normal to expect a problem but decided to concentrate on being happy. Rosie was never far from my thoughts, so maybe that thing they called acceptance was simply that you had to be brave enough to allow yourself to experience happiness whilst accepting and acknowledging that there would always be a part of you that hurt.

Val and I went to watch the medium Colin Fry at a local theatre. It was an entertaining treat and his messages, though not aimed at Val or me, were so specific and detailed they brought enormous comfort. A message he gave to one lady who had lost her partner was that he had come through from spirit to say she must live her life fully and find happiness despite the grief. He would be waiting for her when her time came, but until then she had to live her life and smile. If she received that message from her loved one, then surely Rosie would be there too? I had a duty to her to live as full and happy a life as possible. If roles were reversed and it was me up there, I would certainly want that for my daughter.

Gone to Dance with Rosie
July 2008

Helene was on the phone sounding very worried. Ella was in hospital, having endured a very bad night. She was about to leave her with Mike while she dashed down to her parents' house in Hampshire to wish her dad a happy eightieth birthday. I offered to visit the hospital after lunch and Helene would be back by early evening.

A few minutes later Helene was crying uncontrollably down the phone. "Come quickly to the hospital. Ella has got very much worse. I think this is it."

One of Helene's friends had rushed to her house and driven frantically to take Helene back to Ella's bedside at Wycombe Hospital. I called David. "We have to get to the hospital quick. It's Ella." David told me to meet him at home. I was praying over and over to Rosie, "Rosie, please, please, darling, if this really is Ella's time, please be there to meet her safely, please look after her. I can't believe this is happening, but if you are with her, then she will be safe."

We were caught up in a horrendous traffic jam at Handy Cross roundabout and sat cursing, unable to move. I had a call to my mobile saying, "Come, Carolyn. Please just get here quick." We squeezed into a corner of the packed hospital car park and ran up to ward 7, where another friend of Helene's came running to the entrance to let us in. She grabbed my arm and ran down the corridor to Ella's bed, only to find the curtains were drawn round the cubicle. She looked at me shaking her head. David held back, but I rushed to my dear friend.

Helene was hysterically sobbing. "She's gone. Ella's gone. She has her legs now and she has gone to dance with Rosie." Helene threw herself into my arms and I could only hold her whilst we cried together. Over the next couple of hours, arrangements were made for the family to go to Helen House Hospice in Oxford, where Ella had often stayed for respite breaks. Ella had been ill for so long that Helene already had strong connections with the children's hospice. I also knew Helen House well as I had attended group bereavement support in the early days following Rosie's death. It was a caring and friendly place. There was a special room there where Ella could be laid to rest, and the family would be looked after by experienced hospice staff who supported bereaved parents on a regular basis. Helene, Mike, and their boys already knew many of the staff there.

While the arrangements were being made, we were all on our mobiles, frantically spreading the tragic news. It seemed like a long time until Mike took the boys home to pack some clothes for the week. David and I stayed with Helene, while more friends who were dealing with child death probably for the first time were amazingly calm and had gone into practical mode, dishing out tissues and orange juice. It was reassuring having them there. The adored and precious child of our best friends had gone, just as ours had, and there was nothing anyone could do to take away the savageness of that grief.

They were experiencing endings and we were embarking on new beginnings. It seemed so cruel, and I felt so much guilt that as Ella's life ended my pregnancy was moving forward. I couldn't celebrate my pregnancy when Helene was in the first throes of grief. In any case I was feeling deep sadness for the loss of Ella and huge compassion for our dear friends.

With all this going on, I still had to keep my appointment the next morning at St John and St Elizabeth Hospital in Hampstead to meet an obstetrician I had identified as being the man who could deliver our new baby.

"So, what brings you to this point, this pregnant state?" Nick Morris sat back in his leather swivel chair at his desk, looked at me, and waited. I explained to him how we lost Rosie, and he was clearly shocked. I went on to tell him the saga, the upsetting journey through two failed IVF attempts, the Cyprus trip, and delight at the recent outcome. He seemed genuinely moved and said how happy he was to be delivering the baby for us.

We discussed all the options, and he advised that the baby would probably be delivered by Caesarean section around January 3rd, 2009. As he showed me out, he said, "There is just so much love in you. I am so pleased I have met you. I really like you." I said I felt very confident that he was right for us and so relieved that he was happy to go forward, and that the feeling was mutual. He delivered his babies at the Portland Hospital in London. It was a hospital for the rich and famous and I certainly did not tick either of those boxes, but I checked again with my insurance company and my higher risk pregnancy made it possible for us to arrange the birth there under Nick's expert care.

Helene was holding up well and called me to say she had been offered McFly concert tickets by Helen House for the following evening and she and Mike were bravely taking the boys. I admired her for throwing herself in the deep end. Just one day had passed and she had already chosen to engage with life.

A few days later she was absolutely not okay. "I can't do this." Helene was in a distressed state, her voice shaking, and the funeral was in a few hours.

"Helene, you will do this because you must. We are all beside you and you will survive, but it is going to be very, very tough. I wish there was something I could say which makes it easier, but it's just so hard and there aren't even words to describe it. You will find the courage from somewhere." She was calling me from the little room at Helen House. Ella was beside her. Helene had dressed her in her bridesmaid dress and had placed a brightly coloured Rosie's Rainbow scarf under her feet.

Helene said, "I just said to one of the hospice staff that I put it there because now she will be standing on the rainbow."

I stayed in constant touch with Helene, trying to be helpful. I collected some large glass frames from Homebase, and together with Helene's friend, framed a selection of pictures of Ella. It occurred to me that Helene had a lot more photographs of Ella with her and Mike than I had ever had of Rosie with me. I think I was always the one taking the pictures, so I was rarely in them.

Mazz had called late the previous evening, excited that she had arranged an audition for Ellie for *We Will Rock You* on the morning of the funeral. She hadn't heard about Ella. I asked Ellie whether she wanted to attend the audition. Ellie became dreadfully upset and said that as much as she wanted with all her heart to go to the audition, she needed to be at the funeral to say goodbye to Ella. I called Mazz back and she totally understood and said not to worry. Suddenly I was very emotional and weeping to Mazz down the phone. It was probably the outburst which hadn't happened since Ella died and was waiting to erupt.

Everyone wore pink at Ella's funeral. Although it was unbearably sad and Helene was in such anguish, she tried to smile through her tears, saying, "Ella has her legs now and she is up there on the rainbow with Rosie, dancing, putting on shows, being the star dancer in Rosie's productions."

I thought of the hundreds of shows Ella had attended with us, of watching her as she responded to the music, the stage lights, the sparkle, and the colour despite being non-verbal, unable to do anything for herself, trapped inside a little body which would not do any of the things that children normally do. I tried to count how many times she listened from a front row seat to our Rainbow Choir and never seemed to be bored. Somehow, without ever saying a word or ever walking a step, Ella managed to impact not only the lives of her beloved family and her close friends but also the lives of literally thousands of children for whom Ella had been the inspiration and lynchpin for all the work Rosie's Rainbow did with the special needs children.

It was because of Ella and seeing her response to the magic of music that music became part of the lives of hundreds of children with special needs. And I believed too that, like Rosie, Ella was now truly free. She would be dancing in the pinkest Angelina Ballerina tutu, singing in harmony with Rosie in her latest musical, high kicking, twirling, jumping for joy with her new playmate and old soul mate and planning how to fill mine and Helene's minds with the inspiration for the next Rainbow event. On the day of the funeral, there was even a rainbow to prove that she really had arrived safely.

In the following weeks I tried to be a support for Helene. Their specially adapted big car had immediately been taken away and replaced with a smaller one. Ella's things were being sorted or given away. Helene was being very brave but asked, "How did you get through the last five years without Rosie when I can't even get through one day without Ella?"

I said, "Yes, I have got through the last five years, although I had no idea how, and so you will get through the next five." We shared a few evenings sitting eating too many Doritos and chocolate and watching silly chick flicks. Neither of us could concentrate much, but it helped her pass some time while Mike and David went out for a drink to drown their very real sorrows.

During these few weeks Nick Morris and I were connecting well. He seemed genuinely interested in my case. He described how when he went home to his family after my first appointment with him, he told them my story around the dinner table and all of them were in tears. He updated me on developments since we last met and how he had spoken about me to Professor Steer, an eminent expert on pregnancy in older women. He believed there was a risk of prolapse and described how my womb and literally everything around could just drop out if I tried to deliver naturally. A Caesarean section was the best option. Because there was no known database on cases of my kind, he and Professor Steer had made the decision to start one.

In late July Ellie contracted glandular fever. Three courses of antibiotics didn't ease her painful throat and swollen glands, so I took her to a homeopath. After just two days, her throat cleared up. Whenever she became ill, I freaked out and kept flashing back to the onset of Rosie's illness, the ten courses of antibiotics and the numerous mistakes made at the outset which may have exacerbated the seriousness of her condition. I had taken her to a homeopath too and remembered she had been so poorly she was hardly able to walk from the car to the door. It was not useful nor helpful to relive those days, but they were never far from the surface.

One evening David came home looking distraught. He was driving home through Black Park when a baby deer jumped out of the trees and into the road, where a passing car hit it head-on and killed the poor thing. David got out of the car and pulled the creature to the side of the road and then proceeded to throw up violently and collapse in tears. Five years ago, David had driven Rosie and me to the hospital. It was a day after she had been discharged and we were taking her back to the JR for a blood test. A brown dog ran out onto the M40, narrowly missing our car, and we remembered how upset and how overwrought Rosie had been and how she had screamed for us to avoid it. It was that awful moment. Five years later it was still easy to trigger a painful memory like that.

My pregnancy was advancing towards twenty weeks. It had been an eventful few months and we had been riding on some amazing highs but also some devastating lows. At almost fifty-four my concern was that I was not resting enough, but I was not the type to sit and knit for nine months. I also worried that I wouldn't feel any movement from our baby at the appropriate stage.

We had booked tickets to see Adam performing in *Spamalot* in the West End. We were in a restaurant enjoying a pre-show supper when I felt the baby kick for the first time. Each day after that they became stronger and with each kick my confidence grew along with the size of the baby bump. I was already getting breathless and slightly uncomfortable and wondered whether I should continue to teach dance when our theatre school reopened in September.

Mini Music Makers
August 2008

Helene insisted on being present at the Rosie's Rainbow Mini Music Makers workshop. I knew she would find it very difficult, but she was adamant she wanted to face all these 'firsts' head-on, just as I had in those early days, so my courageous friend did exactly that. Ten pre-school special needs children arrived in small wheelchairs to the workshop together with their siblings and parents, so the place was busy and humming. The morning had been a success. Pauline had written some new songs and engaged all the children with her box of shakers and brightly coloured props. The siblings had loved the tee shirt painting session, which was messy but fun.

Ellie had come along to help, and I was happy that she threw herself into the spirit of the event. For a moment Helene was overcome with the pain of not having Ella there. When we first scheduled the session, Ella had been on the list to attend. Maybe it was through helping Helene with her pain that my own grief lessened or had relocated somehow to a place where I could manage it better. I missed Rosie every day, but at that point I seemed more able to look forward. I would feel movement and fluttering in my stomach and would try to imagine what he or she would look like.

Unmistakeable Bits
August 2008

Ellie, David, and I took the train to Paddington then a taxi to Harley Street for my twenty weeks scan. A quietly spoken man called Gordon was conducting the scan. He ushered us into the ultrasound room. David and Ellie stood nervously beside me as I lay on the bed saying a sort of silent prayer to myself that I really didn't care what sex the baby was but please let it be okay. After the Minnie Music Makers workshop the previous week, I was once again fighting my paranoia that there would be something wrong with our baby and that somehow the 'special needs' workshops had been set up to accommodate my child too.

Gordon pushed the gel and probe around on my tummy as I watched the screen and his expression for any kind of concern. But there was our baby, wriggling and jumping around, and we were all amazed at the clarity of the picture. Gordon was nodding happily. "Well, it is all looking very good indeed, and THAT…" he smiled at me as he circled with the probe over the relevant and unmistakeable bits, "is most definitely a little boy. You have a little boy!"

I was relieved and thrilled and we laughed because the evidence was truly there for all of us to see. I glanced up at Ellie, who was smiling at me. It was hard to read David's expression, but I was transfixed by the picture of our tiny son, Ellie's little brother, so clearly moving about in front of us, his little arms and legs and everything in the right place. He switched to the new 4D ultrasound which made our son look rather like an alien. "To be honest, if you want a clearer and more pleasant 4D picture, you are probably better off waiting till about twenty-eight weeks when there is more flesh. He is very skinny at this stage."

I was delighted and yet had known since the beginning, even before the beginning, that this baby would be a boy.

He handed us the photos and we set off home, trying to absorb this information and prepare for a little boy blue! Ellie and David were very quiet till halfway home when Ellie started joking about names. It seemed to break the silence and the rest of the journey was taken up with our suggestions for names and David coming up with some ridiculous possibilities, such as Ebenezer, Dick Van Dyke, and Horatio. Ellie and I were holding out for Dominic. David wasn't keen on the name, but I guessed we would have to find something we all liked in the nineteen weeks we had left.

As we opened the front door, we could just hear David muttering to himself, "A boy, a son, men in tights, men in tights, Jesus, men in tights!" I knew he was just trying to digest yet another piece of news on this crazy journey I had thrust on all our family.

The psychics' predictions were right, and I was pleased that no one would be able to compare our boy to our beautiful girl because that had always been my worry. Feeling ecstatic that things were still going to plan, it felt even more real and exciting. Arriving home I called Sam, Mum, Helene and texted those who were waiting for the sex reveal. It was a happy day, and all the family were elated.

That evening at the spiritualist church, there was a medium called Tracey working on the platform. She was standing in for another lady who had dropped out at the last minute. Tracey was giving very specific validation to lots of people in the church, but the evening was ending, and I had given up hoping she would have a message for me. Then she suddenly looked at me and said, "The lady in the second row, let me see, one, two, three seats along. Can I come to you, please?" I held my breath as she began.

"I am seeing a country, somewhere on the Eastern Bloc. It looks somewhere like Lithuania, Russia, or somewhere close, and I am to tell you that this country is about to become a part of your family's history!" I laughed out loud as I knew Moldova was near to Lithuania and the donor of my son's egg was indeed from around that area. She went on to describe the lady who was speaking to me from spirit, who had short, curly dark hair and who sounded like my late great aunty. She said she was handing me mistletoe but saying "Mazel tov."

"Strong Jewish connections obviously," said Tracey, who I had never set eyes on in my life but seemed to know things which she said were being channelled through her by spirit. "They are saying that you are doing all the right things, do not be afraid to jump in and go for them. You have a warm heart and give so much to others, now is your time to receive something yourself."

Back in the car, I thanked Rosie with tears streaming down my face, so much so that I had to pull in as I couldn't see clearly enough to drive home.

I had a text from Ellie: *I love you mum, and I'm going to have a little brother called Dom.*

Later I looked up Lithuania on the map and it was very close. There was Lithuania, Belarus, Ukraine, and then Moldova.

Autumn term was back in full swing. I was twenty-three weeks pregnant and over the halfway mark. My tummy felt huge and heavy, and I didn't remember being as uncomfortable last time round, but then it was seventeen years ago, and maybe at age fifty-three I should not expect to feel like jumping round like a twenty-something-year-old. I decided to stop teaching dance and do what was best for the baby. I would never forgive myself if anything went wrong. The kids at school had of course noticed my pregnancy and had taken the news in their stride.

I couldn't remember being kicked so hard in previous pregnancies. Staring at my bump with a sort of hypnotic fascination, I spent ages watching him lurching, rolling, and prodding with his feet, which was reassuring as well as being the most amazing thing in the world. I began looking at nursery fabrics and praying that things would be fine. The lifestyle change would be massive, but I was also very excited that this baby, at almost twenty-four weeks gestation, would soon be viable if he did decide to arrive early.

There was so much to look forward to, although I didn't understand my feelings any better than I had five years ago. The pain and the missing would never leave me and although I felt ecstatic joy at this pregnancy and the forthcoming birth of a baby boy, the truth remained that I would never get over the loss of Rosie. I missed her as much as I always had and for as long as I live, it will always be the same. There was still the same sharp pain every night and questions in my head. Why did she have to leave us? When I closed the curtains at night, I moved a picture of Rosie which has been sitting on my windowsill for the last two years. I couldn't shut her behind them. I felt she was there in that picture.

I was so lucky to be given a second chance, but it was not a second chance really; it was a new beginning which could not diminish my love nor my loss.

A good friend of mine came over for tea. She brought along her two young sons. It quickly became apparent that we would need to child proof our house. The little one who was fourteen months old was into everything. Because we had no toys around, David went up into the loft and brought down a large crate of Rosie and Ellie's Beanies Babies. He didn't mean to upset anyone. The boys played with them for a few hours, which was great, but it was the first time they had been played with since Rosie left us, and it was acutely painful.

In the box were Ellie and Rosie's three exercise books full of Rosie's handwriting with lists of all the Beanies' names, their ailments, and their date of recovery or demise. It brought so many memories flooding back of the happy hours they spent in our old playroom, sorting and building a whole town of Beanies. This used to go for months sometimes. I was in bits, and I wished he had never got them out.

A few weeks later, at twenty-nine weeks, I was now feeling like a beached whale and having trouble sleeping. However, I felt lucky to be able to experience these moments and since this was my final pregnancy decided to appreciate each day despite unpleasant symptoms. Once our baby arrived, I hoped to feel the same way. In the old days when the girls were little, I always wished the time away and looked forward to when they were older – out of nappies, able to talk, to sleep through, and to go to school. I spent so much time rushing, but now I appreciated just how easily lives can be snatched away by some cruel twist of fate, so I longed to savour every moment of this little one's life.

With time for lots of online baby shopping, I ordered a white wooden cot and changing table. Baby blankets and clothes were stacked in neat piles in the nursery wardrobes, and I looked forward to David getting stuck into preparing the room.

Ellie landed the role of Jill, the principal girl in the *Jack and the Beanstalk* panto at Camberley Theatre. She had completed her course, and this was her first job since leaving college. She was contracted for the whole festive season of 2008, so this was going to be a busy Christmas. I hoped to be able to see her in the show before the baby arrived. At twenty she was now almost independent, having graduated from her dance college. She had passed her driving test, so would be able to drive herself to rehearsals and performances.

A scan showed that baby, at just thirty weeks, was already weighing in at four pounds. Because of this, Nick decided to move my delivery date from January 3rd, 2009, back to December 29th, 2008. The baby was in breech position, and his little legs were extended. This meant that there was a 10% chance he could be born with dislocated hips, which would mean that he may be in a splint for six weeks. Although Nick said this was not a big problem and may correct itself anyway, I was suddenly full of anxiety.

In the GP's surgery, I was emotional. I was there for my thirty-two week check-up. I don't know what triggered me, but Dr Scothorne was so lovely and reassuring and I heard myself weeping and confessing my fear that something would be wrong with this baby and how vulnerable I was feeling.

The doctor said it was to be expected because unlike most mums to be, I had experienced the sharp end, with Rosie and with all the sick children on that terrible journey and the thousands of disabled children who we encountered through Rosie's Rainbow Fund. She said that I had seen the worst, just like she and the doctors and nurses and health workers had seen stuff normal people are unaware of, and that because of this it was hardly surprising I was feeling this way. Most *normal* people don't have any idea. They just see a perfect child. They think that the important things of life are how bright the children are, how well they achieve at school, but I knew that ultimately the only thing that mattered was that the child was healthy, happy, and loved. I only wanted this for our new child.

I was truly in nesting mode and had been manically cleaning out cupboards, only putting my feet up when I remembered.

By the end of November, David had finished the nursery. His brother Nigel stayed all week to help with the decorating and it looked fabulous. It was pale blue and white with Peter Rabbit and his friends on the curtains, which were edged in blue and white gingham. The cot and changing table were assembled. Everything looked crisp and fresh, and the room smelled of new paint. How lucky I was to be able to hang little blue and white baby outfits in the new wardrobe on baby blue gingham hangers and stack nappies in the new dresser!

Countdown to Baby
November 2008

A scan revealed that the baby was now six pounds ten ounces. Ellie bought me a Yummy Mummy baby change bag for my birthday.

It was less than a month till the delivery. Candice and Helene were organising a baby shower at my house. They sent me upstairs and as I lay on my bed, I could hear Candice, Helene, Sam, and Ellie preparing the baby shower downstairs. They decorated the living room with blue balloons and Helene made a Beatrix Potter banner spelling *baby shower*, which they hung across the windows. They arranged lots of silly games and had hot chilli con carne simmering away on the hob and a cake decorated with blue smarties.

They sent David off to spend the evening with Helene's husband Mike. Soon my girlfriends and mum arrived. The evening was frivolous and so much fun that it felt good to be happy. I wondered whether Rosie was near and how she would feel in this strange situation.

They put so much effort into the evening and once again I appreciated what good friends I had and felt blessed to have so much love and support on this incredible journey.

There was a game where they had to put their chosen baby's name in a hat, and I had to draw out the names and read them out. The list was so random that I was hysterical with laughter. Otto, Horatio, Ebenezer, Davith. Poor boy. What would he be called in the end? We still had not settled on his name. The evening went too fast, David came home well after midnight, and we eventually fell into bed at 2am.

The following morning, kneeling alone on the living room floor looking at the gorgeous gifts for our baby, I became emotional. This was a happy and hopeful but sad and difficult time. However, we had Ellie, a baby on the way, a beautiful home, my family close by, and amazing friends. There was still a life to be lived as fully as we possibly could.

I noticed an advertisement that Tracey the medium was on at the spiritualist church again and, since it would probably be the last time

I would be able to attend for a while, was compelled to attend on Sunday evening. She came to me last, just as she had before. "This baby," she said to me, "is going be a very special one. The concerns which are running through your head at the moment are unfounded. This baby has YOUR blood coursing through its veins. The spirits are applauding you. You are absolutely on the right path. This time is for you." This was the same lady who a couple of months ago had told me that the Eastern Bloc country somewhere round Ukraine or Lithuania was going to become important in my family's history.

With just two and a half weeks to go, this was the month which would change everyone's lives.

Ellie opened in *Jack and the Beanstalk*. I bought her a small stuffed black and white Daisy the pantomime cow and sent flowers to the theatre so she would receive them on her first performance. We would see the show that weekend. I was so looking forward to watching her and as proud as punch of what she had achieved. Feeling tired and heavy, I wasn't able to do much. David warned me he would probably get all silly and emotional and go to pieces when he met the baby. The last time we met a new-born baby it was 1991, when Rosie arrived, and how could we possibly not be transported back to how we felt in those happy days? There was only hope and joy then. Nowadays we knew so much about what could go wrong and had experienced too much pain to be able to go into this in a carefree way.

A visit to see Nick Morris in the second week of December revealed that my contortionist baby had turned the wrong way up again and so I was called to have a scan. If he remained in breech position, then there was every chance I may be admitted next week.

Ellie had to dress in her Jill panto costume and accompany the boy playing Jack to dish out presents at a Meet and Greet in Frimley Park Hospital. She found it very hard. I hated to see how she still suffered and how being in a hospital setting could trigger grief all over again. At Camberley Theatre they were unaware of her story and wouldn't have had any idea that she was struggling so much. However, in the show she was fabulous. Maybe I was being a 'stage mother', but I was more than proud of her. She was sweet and vulnerable as principal girl, and it was good to watch her doing what she trained for, and seeing her afterwards at the first night party, she was obviously popular with the cast too. She seemed to have struck up a relationship with one of the boy dancers in the cast. She was clearly having a great time.

A scan confirmed that the baby was still in breech, so now we had to wait till Monday to see whether the delivery would be that week. Baby was already seven pounds fourteen ounces, and Nick was also of the opinion that it would be safer to deliver him early than to stand the risk of going into labour and requiring an emergency C-section. We saw the panto again and baby kicked about during the whole show, very obviously responding to the noise and music he was hearing through the walls of his snug haven!

The baby turned himself so he was lying in an oblique position, which meant that I was almost admitted to hospital because there was a risk of the cord prolapsing. Nick Morris monitored me carefully and a few days later at a subsequent scan, it was a huge relief to see that he had turned back the right way and was head down again.

There were twelve days to go, and we were counting down. I visited Amanda, who was having a day off from her parent sessions at John Radcliffe. She gave me a breastfeeding lesson with a baby doll. Sitting on the bed in her home treatment room, she showed me how to tuck the baby doll under my arm so he could suckle easily. I tried to imagine what the reality would be like. I had bottle fed both Ellie and Rosie, having struggled with breastfeeding and had given up after just a couple of days. I wondered if things might have turned out different if I had persisted and breastfed Rosie. Would she have been more protected? The *what ifs* served no useful purpose, but what if?

It was now just a waiting game, so this was going to be a surreal Christmas. David gift-wrapped a present for the baby in Christmas paper and placed it in a prominent position under the Christmas tree. The gift tag read *to my son*. It touched me, and it was comforting to know that David was a big softie. In fact, he had bought him a toy tool kit. I had lots of texts and phone calls asking for news and updates. Nick saw us for the last time before the birth. Smiling, he said he would look forward to seeing us on the big day.

Christmas Day was manic as we ended up with a big crowd for lunch, but everyone enjoyed it. Helene, Mike, and the boys joined us and got through the day as well as they possibly could. For them it was their first Christmas without Ella, for us our sixth without Rosie, but somehow they kept smiling all day and I think because it was so busy here, it helped them through. Rowan and Sasha brought their Nintendo Wii, which kept them occupied all day long. David cooked, and I did what I could, although I looked and felt so heavy. Ellie loved her presents and all in all the pain felt less than usual, probably because we were distracted by the imminent arrival.

We managed another trip to Ellie's panto just a day before my admission. Ellie had plenty of supporters cheering her on. It was good to watch her again knowing it was probably the last time before my own opening night. There was just one day to go, and I was very nervous. This was the culmination of five years of planning, hope, dashed hope, longing, and belief that this could really happen – and now it really was.

Suddenly I felt totally isolated because David went into one of his silent moods. After months of him being so supportive, I reasoned that it was just his uncertainty and trepidation, but with only a few hours to go, when I needed 100% support, he seemed very distant. I was afraid of everything, afraid of the C-section and mostly of what I might feel when the baby was born and if I would love him like I loved my other two children and whether I could cope and whether I had made the right choices.

The last few jobs were done. My hospital bag had been checked at least a dozen times, so I cleared up again then forced myself to go to bed, although I couldn't sleep.

Dominic – Rosie's Gift
December 2008

On the morning of December 29th, David put my bag in the boot. It was 5.30am. Taking a final look at the house and noting that on our return I would be carrying an added appendage, we headed up the M40, arriving early at the Portland Hospital. I was a bag of nerves as we entered the reception. We were shown to our room. I had received a list of items to pack, which I took out of my holdall, placing a photo of Rosie by my bed. All my checks were carried out before I changed into a surgical gown and long green hospital socks. My nerves were getting the better of me. With my 'nil by mouth' stomach churning, I struggled to sit still or even breathe.

At 7.30am the porter escorted us in the lift down to the operating theatre. My legs shook and my hands were freezing as we walked to the door of the theatre. What a theatrical production this was going to be!

The operating theatre felt as chilly, white, and clinical as I did. There was a clock on the wall which would log the time of the birth. The bed stood in the centre and various nurses were moving about, talking quietly to each other, donning gloves and masks, and checking equipment.

I was relieved to see Nick, who greeted us warmly. He was in his scrubs and a mask, and his demeanour was a little more serious than usual.

David was fine until I was told to sit on the operating table, legs over the side, and the anaesthetist prepared the long needle for the epidural which was about to be inserted into my lower back. I closed my eyes tight and waited for the jab. The next thing I heard was Nick in a jovial tone,

"David, you are looking like a nervous wreck. You look as though you are about to faint. Can I suggest you come into the next room with me, and we can talk about football?"

David followed on his heels like an obedient puppy, and I was left with the nurses and the anaesthetist.

"You must keep perfectly still while we insert the needle. Soon you will be all numb." A nurse in scrubs was holding my shoulder and I felt the jab and tried not to wince and shake. It was a strange sensation, and I no longer had any feeling. I lay on the bed as the numbness spread through my body. I prayed I wouldn't feel any pain. The nurses prepared me for the Caesarean section.

Nick reappeared with David, who, clearly petrified, was instructed to stand at the top of the bed while a large screen-like curtain was erected across my stomach so I couldn't see what was happening. Nick was asking if I could feel anything. He was tapping my leg, but I didn't experience much physical sensation.w

"You will be aware of a lot of activity and pulling and pushing but no pain. I will see you shortly," he said as he disappeared behind the curtain. The nurse was holding my hand and I couldn't see David, which was probably just as well since he had turned as white as the walls. I could hear metal instruments, nurses, and the anaesthetist responding to Nick's instructions. The nurse was talking to me, although I couldn't concentrate on what she was saying. It felt as though someone was rummaging around deep inside me, but it didn't hurt. It seemed like an eternity until Nick said, "It won't be long now."

And then he was here! I saw our baby being lifted out of me and into the world. His first cry was strong and gutsy, and Nick looked over the curtain holding up the baby and said, "Here he is. Here is your little boy." I looked at the clock and it was 8.55am. The baby was weighed, measured, and swaddled securely in a white hospital blanket.

Rosie's gift was placed on me with his head in the crook of my arm. Our new baby boy was here. With tears streaming down my face, I acknowledged that these were tears of relief and joy, not of grief and pain. "We've done it, David. He's really here." I was crying and sobbing and laughing. Our eight-pound, ten-ounce bundle of promise for the future opened his eyes wide and looked at me and from that moment on he had my heart. Here was the result of five years of determination and refusal to give up on living. Here lay the proof that all things were possible. Here I was at the grand old age of fifty-four, a proud mother of a healthy new-born baby son.

I held him as they sewed me up and wheeled me out into recovery whilst David went off to make phone calls to Ellie, Sam, Mum, and his brothers. I am not sure how much time passed, but when I was ready, I was wheeled back up to our room, where the baby was placed in a crib by my bed with an identity label edged in blue with his arrival date, family name, and gender stuck to the side.

Ellie, Mum, and Sam visited us at the hospital. It was pure magic watching Ellie peeping into his crib for the very first time and holding her brother Dominic's tiny hand in wonder.

Carolyn, David and baby Dominic

The nurses at the Portland looked after me and Dominic for five days, showed me how to bath him, and took him into the maternity wing nursery at night so I could recover and sleep. Nick was happy with my progress and proud that he had safely delivered the baby, achieving a successful outcome in unusual circumstances. Dominic and I welcomed in the new year.

The year 2009 was the beginning of a new era for us all. We were finally discharged on January 2nd. David and I took Dominic home. He was five days old.

Baby Bliss
January 2009

Dominic Joseph Orlando had rosy cheeks, lots of hair, and blue eyes, and we had fallen head over heels in love with him. He brought David, Ellie, and me a future. This little human being had surely been sent by Rosie. Here he was in my arms in his Peter Rabbit nursery which I had dreamed about all those years ago.

When I looked at him, held him, heard his little squeaks, smelled his delicious milky baby smell, and rubbed my cheek on his silky downy hair, I felt peace and contentment which I never thought I could experience again. I recalled that day at the farm when, overwhelmed by the depths of despair and mourning, I had felt so jealous of that pig and her new piglets.

Dominic was a placid baby. He possessed a calm aura and I believe he had met Rosie and she had chosen him to be the one to bring us the joy I never thought possible to feel again. Every moment was precious, and I was totally content to just be with him and drink in each second, savour it and make it last forever.

David was cooking for us each night and trying to process what had happened within our family. He was struggling with guilt that our son was only here because Rosie was not. We would always experience sadness. This perhaps was the meaning of acceptance.

I managed to breastfeed and relished the skin-to-skin closeness with Dominic. We had a string of visitors and well-wishers and hundreds of gorgeous celebratory messages on Facebook, by email, and on numerous cards which arrived by post. Gifts were flooding in, and it seemed that our whole world of family, friends, and people we knew were waiting for Dominic. It was five years since the day I heard her voice in my head. That day in the garden in the summer of 2003, when mounded in grief and pain, I heard Rosie say, "Don't talk about it. Do it."

I would never stop missing and aching for Rosie, but this little miracle boy marked a new beginning for all of us and I felt truly blessed.

On We Go
2012

Dominic was a happy child. His mop of golden curls and placid nature endeared him to everyone. He developed a strong bond with Ellie, although there was a twenty-year age gap. He was everything I could have wished for and more and over the next couple of years, I relished revisiting the world of mother and toddler groups, nursery school, and the new circle of friends who readily accepted me even though I was a much older mum.

We were working parents and so we employed Amy, a perfect nanny whom he adored. Amy brought order, routine, happy outings, and so much more besides.

Redroofs school was busy and the charity running smoothly. We added another music therapist to our charity team. Andy's outstanding ability to use music to connect with the children we supported meant he quickly became a firm favourite among the children at John Radcliffe, who called him Andy the music man.

*Joanne Froggatt and Carolyn join music therapist Andy Stevens
at John Radcliffe Hospital*

We invited an ex-Redroofs pupil, Joanne Froggatt, to join our roster of Rosie's Rainbow Fund patrons. During her time at Redroofs as an unassuming but clearly gifted budding actress, she had landed her first TV role in *The Bill*. She remained regularly in touch and as genuine and down to earth as she had always been. Jo was making a name for herself as an exceptional actress, receiving a lot of media attention in her role as Anna Bates in *Downton Abbey*. She happily accepted the role as patron and made visits to John Radcliffe Hospital, where she spent time chatting with the children and parents on the wards, and her generosity and kindness brightened their days.

In September 2012, after a happy year in the school nursery, Dominic moved into the reception class. He was now almost four and a bright, sociable child, loving everything about school, especially the play dates and deepening friendships. Our home was once again full of the chaos of kids' paraphernalia, toys, clutter, and chicken nuggets. Together with my new circle of mums from Dom's school, we took the kids on park visits, outings, and picnics.

Ellie and Matt decided to get married. They had been a couple since they met during panto and now planned a big white wedding. We booked a stunning venue and were choosing the caterers and music. It was a good time in so many ways, but David and I were struggling with our own marriage. It was clear that that we were drifting further apart and leading almost separate lives.

Dominic adored his father and was the reason I tried literally anything to stave off a separation, although David kept suggesting it. I chose denial, thinking that if I avoided the issue, maybe it would go away. Trying to ignore the situation was stressful, but I internalised the misery. My stomach was always in knots with the worry of it. Surely having weathered so many years of far worse grief and pain, we could stay together for the sake of the family.

Another Ending
November 2013

After twenty-six years of marriage, David met someone else, and in November 2013 finally moved out. Despite all our efforts we became one of those high statistics of couples who split after the death of a child. We had hung on through ten years of grief, both shattered into a trillion pieces after Rosie's death. This was another sort of grief and loss, painful and lonely. The stress left me depleted and exhausted.

A Rosie's Rainbow Fund ball was scheduled for just a week after David left. The trustees and I had a lot to organise. Gathering my strength with their help and with some truly wonderful friends providing me with tissues and a whole lot of emotional support, I went out and purchased a new teal ball gown and booked a cut and colour at the hairdressers, ready to 'go to the ball'.

Lucy Benjamin sat beside me at the event and said, "You look amazing, my darlin'. You won't have any trouble finding a new man with your figure!" Her down to earth comment meant a lot to me. My wild, overabundant curly frizz had been tamed and she remarked that having my hair under control made me feel I was in control of my life and that I should keep it like that. I decided to treat myself to a weekly hairdo and to do whatever it took to feel better.

I began a new chapter as a separated single parent, and it was okay. Dominic, aged five, was young enough to adapt to the change and saw his dad at regular intervals. He seemed unphased and I maintained a smile in front of him. David and I started divorce proceedings and life fell into a new pattern.

Robin's Diagnosis
December 2013

Through the turmoil of our separation, the wider family provided a stalwart support system. Our family drew close, and both my brothers Robin and Ludo would call regularly, offering a listening ear.

One day at a family get-together at my mum's house, Robin had fallen asleep on the sofa. He was not looking good. We were all concerned as he was having trouble remembering things, often struggling to complete a sentence. He underwent tests and to our horror was diagnosed with an advanced brain tumour. The shocking test result of a malignant grade 4 glioblastoma came with the grim prognosis of a life expectancy of eighteen months to a maximum five years in very rare cases.

Robin Keston and Carolyn

Robin was the cleverest in our family. He had an astute business brain and had made a financial success of everything he did. He also had a reputation as a world class poker player and had achieved a top ranking in the world championships. How was this fair? How was it right that my mother, after all she had been through dealing with the loss of Rosie, her granddaughter, now had to find the resources to witness her younger son's physical decline? It was clear that our family had to deal with this somehow. His children, Emily, L-J, and Molly-May, were young adults, but this did not make it any easier for them. Once again, the whole family had to face serious illness head-on. It hit everyone hard, including his ex-wife Helen and his new partner. Robin's treatment commenced. He dealt with each operation and treatment with courage, resilience, and a sense of humour.

Ellie's Wedding
June 2014

Ellie and Matt married in June. Ellie was a stunning bride in the grand summer wedding at Hedsor House in Taplow. It was a bittersweet day. Ellie had chosen to have all her cousins and a few best friends, totalling no less than twelve bridesmaids, who she dressed in soft pink and pale green, adorned with summer flowers arranged with artistic flair by my sister-in-law Fiona. Dominic, as the only page boy and ring bearer, took his role very seriously. It was clear that Ellie had chosen a large cohort of bridesmaids to fill the massive void where Rosie wasn't. Rosie would no doubt have been her chief bridesmaid and there was an unspoken heartache amid the smiles and happiness of the day. Robin had made a huge effort to attend the wedding despite being in poor health. We were all there – except Rosie.

Addressing the guests at the speeches, I spoke of how I knew Rosie would be so proud of her beautiful sister. As I said her name, everyone gasped and turned to the window. In true Rosie style she somehow made her own appearance right on cue. A huge double rainbow had appeared right over the venue. All the wedding guests rushed to the door to witness it and we wept and laughed as I said, "She's here. I knew she wouldn't miss it." The photographer, who was completely bemused and confused by all the blubbing guests, managed to grab his camera and capture the rainbow, so it is there for all to see in the photograph album, and we have no doubt that Rosie attended her big sister's wedding.

A Point of Light
November 2014

At the end of 2014 I was thrilled to be awarded a Point of Light certificate from the ex-prime minister David Cameron. This amazing accolade was presented in recognition of outstanding individual volunteers – Points of Light – in our country who do extraordinary things in the service of others. David Cameron's letter stated I was an example of service and dedication, making our communities stronger and our country a better place. There were radio interviews and news features, and I was very proud to talk about my daughter and how she works through me, always feeding me the next idea or initiative. In my mind Rosie was the winner of the Point of Light. I was the channel through which she worked her magic. We worked as a team.

Tabitha Rose
August 2015

The following year Ellie and Matt became parents, and I became a grandma. Ellie and I spent hours discussing names. New beginnings were so exciting. This perfect little person was named Tabitha Rose – after Rosie, of course. Seeing Ellie hold her daughter for the first time was quite emotional and I ached, wishing Rosie was there in her role as aunty. Ellie discovered the power of mother love and adored her baby daughter. For the rest of 2015, it was all about baby clothes and nappies and Ellie and Matt finding their feet as first-time sleep-deprived parents.

One Lump or Two
March 2016

It was a Saturday evening, and after a busy day, I had put Dom to bed and flopped onto the sofa in my living room. I began idly surfing the TV channels for something to watch. The house was quiet. The movie *My Sister's Keeper* had just started. I settled down to watch it. Realising I had read this Jodi Picoult book and knew the story, I wondered why I decided it was a good idea. Since Rosie's death I had carefully avoided films or TV programmes about hospitals and medical stuff. Anything like that propelled me back to a dark place with images of medication and frightened children being fitted with cannulas.

Despite these memories I did not switch channels but continued watching images of bald children, chemotherapy, and lots of sickness, resulting in the death of a child at the end of the film.

Then I locked up, switched off the TV, and went to bed. A horrible nightmare involving hospital, illness, and disease woke me up. It was early morning. It was just a night terror after watching the film, but I was shaky and dripping with sweat.

I climbed out of bed, told myself to calm down and stop being overdramatic. Standing in front of the mirror of my dressing table, I told my reflection, "Just breathe and don't be stupid!"

Then I heard the voice. It was loud and clear as a bell and it was without emotion, but it was a voice I did not recognise, and it spoke straight into my right ear as clearly as if someone had walked into my room and delivered a matter-of-fact message about the day's arrangements. Whoever or whatever it was simply said,

"It's your turn for cancer now!"

That was it, just six words, and I remember turning my head sharply towards the voice to see who spoke and thinking who the hell was that?

In that instant I put my right hand over my heart because it was pounding, and I felt it. IT was there! Hard, no bigger than a thumb nail, round like a stone and undeniably real. I had a lump on my left breast.

It was a Sunday morning, just two hours ahead of one of the biggest dates in our school calendar, Redroofs scholarship auditions day. At 9.30am sixty talented kids, and their nervous parents, arrived from all over the UK to sing and dance for a place at our school. I was one of the judges on the panel and needed smiling positivity and my wits about me.

So, I dressed Dominic, waved him off brightly as he drove off for a day out with his father, and put on my professional persona. Arriving at school, I put my fear into a box and spent the day smiling and doing my job.

Next morning, I called the doctors surgery for an emergency appointment. The receptionist handed me a form to fill in.

Under the heading *Give brief explanation of symptoms*, I wrote, *Have lump on left breast.*

My favourite doctor was on duty, and she examined me.

"I am going to refer you to Ms Shrotria at Princess Margaret in Windsor. She is an excellent consultant and surgeon and does a very neat job."

My heart was pounding.

"What job? What neat job?"

I made an appointment for the next day.

Ms Sunita Shrotria called me to her consulting room. This serene lady smiled gently and sent me to undress behind a curtain.

I was lying on her bed, then sitting up, arms in the air, then outstretched as she prodded and pressed and pushed her fingers around under my arm. All the while I was staring at her expression, searching for clues.

"I think," she said quietly, "it may just be some matted breast tissue, but all the same, we will send you for tests. You have some puckering of the skin, and we need to check it out."

I felt relieved, hoping maybe I would be one of many women for whom breast lumps and bumps turn out to be benign. Feeling frightened, I couldn't eat and shed half a stone in a week.

At the Parapet breast clinic in Windsor, I was greeted by a radiologist who recognised me from many years ago when I had taught her daughter to dance. "Are you okay with me doing this?" she asked.

"Yes, I'm fine," I mumbled as I lay on the bed.

She smeared some gel on the stick and moved it about over both breasts. She was concentrating hard on the monitor, and I was concentrating hard on her face. A nurse was standing by my left shoulder.

The radiologist was staring at something on the screen, but I couldn't work out what she was thinking. Why was the nurse standing next to me rubbing my shoulder? What was going on?

"Have you seen anything?" I blurted out.

"Just a minute," said the radiologist quietly, "then we will discuss."

She was measuring a black spot on the screen. And then... another?

"There is something there, yes," she said.

"What is it, please?"

"It looks suspicious."

"In your opinion, what do you think?" I heard a tremor in my voice.

"In my opinion it looks like a cancer. In my opinion it is not good, and we need to get you a mammogram and a biopsy as soon as possible."

A wave of nausea overcame me, and I tried not to cry.

The nurse still rubbing my arm said, "Let it out. It's okay to let it out."

In the same way as I had felt when Rosie had been so terribly ill in intensive care, I suddenly felt I was outside my body and looking down on this woman lying on the bed who was me. I was still lying down and shaking.

I was back in that moment when Rosie had a cardiac arrest and being told to breathe into a paper bag by her nurse. I think this is what happens when shock is too much and what humans do when the truth is too hard to tolerate. I chose to temporarily remove myself from me. After the scan I was sent away with a list of appointments for a multitude of tests. There were MRI scans, a mammogram, and

CT scans, with a lot of medics injecting dyes into my increasingly sore breast.

During these early frightening days, I couldn't eat, sleep, or think straight. Then I received a phone call from the secretary asking me to see Ms Shrotria.

"Why?"

She was being very careful about what she said. It was a pattern I was sure they dealt with every day. Petrified patients processing life-changing news.

"Ms Shrotria will discuss everything with you."

Amanda offered to accompany me. As a lynchpin of our Rosie's Rainbow Fund team, she was well used to dealing with the worst trauma. She was in a good position to explain medical jargon to me. "I will come and bring a notebook so we can write everything down."

In the waiting room at Princess Margaret Hospital, I was sick with worry. Amanda tried to make conversation to distract me. I couldn't concentrate on what she was saying, although thankful she was there. Not many patients in that waiting room looked as scared as me, and I was trembling as we went to the consulting room.

Jane the breast care nurse was sitting with us, and Amanda opened her notebook.

"So, we have here the result of the tests and this is how it looks," Ms Shrotria said. "We have one tumour which is as big as a thumb nail. It is ER positive."

"I think that's good, isn't it? Doesn't that mean that it will be treated with radiotherapy? Can I just have a lumpectomy?"

"The other tumour…" she was saying.

"Another tumour? What other tumour?"

"There is another tumour. A second one. It is on the same breast but in a different place, beneath the left nipple and deeper inside. It is…" she paused, "a little bigger."

"What do you mean?"

"The result of the biopsy for these shows that this is an HER 2 tumour. This means that chemotherapy would be a given."

My stomach churned. Holding my head in my hands, I was screaming inside. No, not chemo. This was everything I had been dreading.

"I don't want to die. I need to see my son grow up."

Ms Shrotria was calm and measured. "You are not going to die. We are going to get you through this. We will need to do a full left breast mastectomy because of where the tumours are and because of the nature of the HER 2 tumour, which is an aggressive tumour, and we will not take the chance. When we perform the mastectomy, we will also take out the sentinel lymph node to ensure that nothing has spread into the lymphatic system. This is a normal procedure. Once we have the result of that, we will then be able to sort out a treatment plan. So, I will send you tomorrow for a sentinel lymph node tracing. They will inject more dye and prepare the area for me to take out a lymph node when we operate."

Jane the breast care nurse, who had been sitting quietly at the side of the room, was very kind and did her best to reassure me. I was a heap. My world was closing in as I realised that from this day on I was now a cancer patient. I was blubbering and confused when the breast care nurse put her arm round me.

"I have a seven-year-old son and a family who depends on me. After Rosie died, I hoped the bad things would stop, but they keep happening."

She said quietly, "You will get through this. You know, I don't often share this, but I am going to share with you. I lost my daughter too." She then told me her sad story and we knew we understood each other.

In the hospital car park, in Amanda's passenger seat, I cried.

"I don't want to lose my hair. I don't want to be like the bald children in the Jodi Picoult movie. I don't want to be stared at, labelled as a woman dying with cancer. I don't want cancer to define me and turn me into someone I don't recognise."

Amanda drove me home, where we relayed the bad news to Ellie,

Mum, Sam, and the rest of the family. I tried to soften it for my mum, but there was not much hope of covering up the truth. Two of her children with cancer. This was unbelievable. Ellie went into coping mode and asked David to take Dominic for a few days.

One of my closest friends was the mother of one of Dom's best friends from his school. Surangi was a GP and was shocked when I told her my news.

Surangi printed off a lot of information on breast cancer and brought it over for me to digest. Her input, wisdom, and medical knowledge produced some comfort. In between her own surgeries, she would talk to me and offer suggestions. The rest of my circle of mums from Dom's school heard the news and rallied round, offering to look after Dominic and provide practical help wherever they could. How the hell was I going to tell Dominic what was happening?

Next day there were more appointments. In a large hospital I had never visited before, they injected dye into my breast.

Once again, since I was lucky enough to be a member of the school's private health scheme, I could be operated on quickly. Surgery was booked for March 10th, just eight days after I had found the lump.

The day before the operation, I went to Marks and Spencer to purchase what I needed for the hospital. I found a pair of pink satin front-opening pyjamas. Although they were attractive, I hated them and promised myself that as soon as I was better, they were going straight out of my life. I called them my cancer pyjamas. All I could think was get this cancer off me, get it OUT!

Ellie, Matt, and baby Tabitha moved into my house so Ellie could be on hand to help. They moved in for the duration, taking over the top floor of the house.

On March 10th Sam drove me to the hospital for my mastectomy. I had to remind myself that although this was traumatic, I would be leaving cancer free. Once in my room I unpacked my case and, as usual, placed a small picture of Rosie on the bedside table. Once again I was instructed to put on surgical socks and an operating gown.

Ms Shrotria came in to draw an arrow on my left arm and a felt tip line where the cut would be. The anaesthetist introduced himself. He was friendly and reassuring. Then it was time to go down to theatre. I walked down with a nurse, lay on a bed just outside the operating theatre, and prayed I would be asleep fast. The anaesthetist clad in scrubs first gave me an injection then placed a mask over my face as I stared at the lights.

Then it was over. Everything was blurry, muffled, and I could hear voices and then nothing. I woke up back in my room. Sam was there, but I was on morphine and a cocktail of other drugs. I spent a few days heavily bandaged and recuperating whilst my family and a few friends visited to lighten my mood.

It was good to come home. I spent the first few days propped up in bed or in my lounge surrounded my cushions, nursed beautifully by Amanda and Ellie while dear friends popped by with flowers and food parcels. Dominic's old nanny Amy, who had left us when Dominic started nursery, drove all the way from Newcastle not once but three times to help with Dominic. I realised how very fortunate I was to have a support network like this.

There were hospital visits and then the removal of the bandages. I was terrified about seeing the wound for the first time. The team of breast care nurses were brilliant and patient with me. They had seen it all before, but it was horribly difficult. Closing my eyes, she carefully eased off the heavy bandaging, revealing a wide horizontal wound. My breast had gone, but so, I hoped, had the cancer. Handing me a mirror, the nurse was reassuring, saying the scar would fade over time and it was looking as good as it could at that stage.

The soreness improved and just six days after the mastectomy, Candice drove me to Home Sense to get me out of the house. I was chuffed to be back in the real world and Candice was full of encouragement, although I had to sit down on their 60% off sofas a few times.

A few days later I was introduced to my oncologist, Dr Narottam

Thanvi. I liked him immediately. He was charming and so knowledgeable. He was also understanding. "We will get you well. I know you have a son and I have a son of the same age. I will look after you." He laid out my treatment plan. "In a few weeks we will begin chemotherapy, once a week for eighteen weeks, and Herceptin injections, which will treat the HER 2. It is a successful new treatment for this type of cancer."

I had a few weeks to get accustomed to the idea of having chemo. Fear of losing my hair was now a reality. I began researching a thing called the Paxman cold cap, which could prevent me going bald. It worked for some women, so I was definitely giving this a go.

I had to find a wig option as a backup plan. My sister-in-law Fiona had worked for many years making and styling wigs at the Royal Shakespeare Company in Stratford-Upon-Avon and was possibly the most creative and comforting Mother Earth type person on the planet. I called her. "Don't you worry," she said. "I have good connections and I will send you to the best wigs. We can order one and I will make it perfect for you."

Going to my weekly blow dry at the hairdresser suddenly became extra precious. Knowing it was a luxury which was about to stop made me sensitive and tearful. Gaynor, my hairdresser, was like a counsellor to me for those few weeks. She promised to help with the wig too. "Trust me, my darling, you will be fine. I will come over and help too."

A few weeks later Fiona and Cordelia, my niece, arrived at the house bearing a large rose-covered box. The last time she had done my hair had been at Ellie's wedding and this was rather a different challenge, but in true Fiona fashion she laid everything out on the table in my conservatory and set to work. Ellie watched and took notes as she pinned my hair into a French plait and covered it with a wig cap. The plan was to go to Gaynor and have my hair cut short before chemo started so the wig would fit better.

My first reaction when she lifted the wig from the box was that it was all wrong, but when she put it on my head, it looked close to the real thing. Out came her scissors and she shaped it so it looked just like mine as Ellie and Cordelia offered funny comments and lightened the mood. "It's really good," said Ellie. "I mean really good."

I looked like me, just tidier.

Welling up with tears and thanking God I had family in all the right places, gone was the fear that I may look like King Lear in the play Fiona was working on.

Gaynor called round after work. She agreed the wig looked great as Fiona had chopped and shaped it. Sam called with a bunch of roses and there was almost a party atmosphere.

Later I braved it to the local TK Maxx wearing the wig to gauge any reaction or stares from shoppers. I was relieved that no one seemed to notice even though I was aware of a big bulge at the back where Fiona had plaited my very thick hair.

An email arrived that evening from Gina, my Jewish actress friend and patron of Rosie's Rainbow. It was just a line, *How are the sheitels?* I laughed and said, *Even my Jewish roots wouldn't be showing with this new sheitel.*

"I think I can do this," I said out loud. I was resigned to baldness and feeling quite upbeat.

Over the next few days, I tried to tell myself that thousands of women get through chemo and all that goes with it. I kept Googling women on YouTube with their hair dropping in clumps, which was not conducive to peaceful dreams. I read up on the cold cap and was going to try to tolerate it even though I discovered it was uncomfortable and you should literally expect brain freeze eighteen times over. Oh, and it didn't always work!

Dire Notice
April 2016

Dr Thanvi was running late. A blonde-haired lady followed me into the oncology waiting room. She looked very worried, and I recognised the expression of silent fear on her face. We immediately struck up a conversation. She was a month behind me on the cancer journey and due for an operation the following week. Carrie and I became instant buddies. We compared notes. It was very clear we were on similar paths. She was scared about the same things, and I immediately felt less isolated. We exchanged mobile numbers, planned to look out for each other, and became friends.

Dr Thanvi had prepared a plan. "On Monday you will have your first Herceptin injection. This goes into your thigh every three weeks for one year. Then on Tuesday it will be your first day of chemotherapy." He prescribed Paclitaxel, which is a gentler chemo, as the cancer had not spread into my lymph nodes. The breast care nurse urged me to get my hair cut very short in preparation for the cold cap. She was very clear that any extra weight in my hair would result in it breaking off and increased the likelihood of it falling out altogether. I called Gaynor and booked in for a cut. "We can do this, my darling." Gaynor's positivity was comforting. The sight of the scissors was not.

"Don't you worry. It will look beautiful, trust me."

She chopped the back first and I could feel the cold air on the back of my neck. The curls were over the salon floor and there was no going back. Gaynor gave me some gentle shampoo products, but I left feeling bereft and not like me.

"You look weird," said Dominic.

"Thanks, Dom, I feel weird too."

"Mummy, did you get your dire notice?"

"Yes, my darling, I got my diagnosis."

I had summoned up the guts to break the news to him a few days before. I was worried that he would be traumatised if I went bald, so the breast care nurse gave me a book called *Mummy's Lump*, designed for telling small children about mums who have cancer. We curled up on the sofa and read it together. At the end he laughed long and hard and said, "That will be so funny, and I will tell all my friends and they'll think that's funny too. Mummy, if you go bald, will you take the wig off at night?" In true seven-year-old boy style, he had already told his class that I was going to go bald and that they could all come and have a look. Brilliant!

With a Little Help from My Friends
April 2016

On Monday, April 25th, Candice picked me up to accompany me to the hospital. Glad that she was with me, we climbed the stairs to the first-floor oncology unit.

It was like a large lounge with comfortable reclining armchairs, where I was greeted by a friendly nurse. Candice chattered away nineteen to the dozen with anyone within earshot. Other patients arrived. Many greeted each other like old friends, having forged lasting friendships through this shared experience. Some had family or friends with them, some came alone and tapped away on their mobiles while the nurses hooked them up onto drips and hung bags of chemotherapy drugs on their stands. Many were bald, some had scarves or hats, and some had wigs.

It was as though I was part of a rehearsal for a TV soap that I had been cast in but had somehow arrived in the wrong play. Whether I liked it or not, I was now part of this community who had been thrown together to act out this drama.

A friendly lady with a neat bob sitting next to me struck up a conversation.

"You actually look really well, and you've kept your hair," I said.

"Oh no, I'm on the end of my chemo and it's not my hair." She laughed. I was coming to terms with the fact that not all cold cap treatments work and that I may be bald very shortly.

She continued, "I am totally bald under here. It's taken me ages to be able to even look at myself in the mirror with no hair. I never let anyone see my naked head!"

I was ushered into a side room and a nurse administered the Herceptin jab into my thigh. I had to wait six hours in case of any side effects, but it was all good and there were none. Candice was deep in conversation with a musician who was accompanying his wife on her treatment day. He laughed at me as I had a fitting for my cold cap.

"It looks like something worn by a '60s band singing 'I'm the urban spaceman, baby.'" He chuckled.

It was a large green rubber cap with an outer helmet which fitted very tightly over the top. Attached to it was a long blue tube resembling an elephant's trunk. It was strange that we were able to laugh when I was expecting to do anything but. Although it was the beginning of the dreaded chemo and treatment journey, in a weird sort of way, it was quite a good day.

That evening Ellie presented me with a homemade book bound with a pink ribbon and entitled *With a Little Help from My Friends*. Inside were pages of messages of support, poems written by my friends with affirmations, jokes, and insightful letters, and promises of fun things to do when treatment was over. This gift from my caring daughter made me laugh hysterically and blubber like an idiot. I was really feeling the love from all these amazing people.

Next morning was the first day of chemotherapy and I arrived at the hospital feeling anxious. In my armchair the nurse inserted the cannula into my right hand.

"You will be okay. We will look after you, so please don't worry."

"I know you've had your hair cut, but you still have quite a lot of hair," she said as she used a large spray bottle to soak my curls before plastering it with hair conditioner to keep the moisture in. I felt the cold water running down my back and then the inner layer of the cold cap was tugged firmly over my head. With the second layer strapped firmly and quite uncomfortably in position and secured tight under my chin, I immediately felt the freezing cold air as it pumped into the cap. If you think of a large ice cream swallowed too fast, it was like that sort of brain freeze but compounded a hundred times. After a few minutes I was numb with the cold, unable to feel anything much. My hair and my head were literally frozen solid.

The nurse switched on the TV to try to calm my nerves. *Loose Women* was on, and I was distracted by a lively musical theatre actress who was discussing her recent breast cancer diagnosis. I was amazed that she was working through her chemotherapy while performing in *Hairspray*. She had agreed to do the interview in the hope that she could reach even one woman going through the same thing and show them that it was possible to survive this. "It is all about PMA – positive mental attitude," she said.

"Thank you," I whispered to her on the screen. "If you can do it, so can I."

The nurse hooked up the chemo infusions together with an anti-sickness emetic and Piriton. I surrendered myself to the inevitable and watched it drip through the bag, down the pipe, and into me. Feeling very cold, I decided to purchase a heated blanket to warm me up for the next seventeen treatments. Apparently, I dozed off halfway through a bowl of tomato soup and jacket potato and when I woke up the soup had been removed and only the dregs of chemo remained in the bag. I had to stay another hour to 'defrost' because if you take the cap off too soon, your hair could simply snap off. When they removed the cap, my head resembled a walnut whip. Then I went home with a damp head but feeling okay. The first day of chemo was over. It was almost a breeze, albeit a very cold one.

Over the next few weeks, I tolerated the weekly chemo and obsessively checked the sink and bedclothes every day for falling hair. There certainly was some, but I was managing to retain about 60% and I had a lot to start with.

Carrie looked out for me, and we sat beside each other whenever we could. We became true cancer buddies, looking forward to seeing each other every week, when we shared our cake and problems. I learned the shocking statistic that one in eight women in the UK develop breast cancer and read somewhere it is believed that those coping with a bad relationship are more likely to develop the disease. Disease is triggered by Dis-Ease, and I came to realise that the twisting feeling I used to get in my gut when things were bad, during the lowest points of IVF and more recently through the divorce, eventually made me very ill.

Some days were harder than others. Feeling tired or slightly sick became normal, but I got through it, put on a brave face for Dominic, who was living as near normal routine as possible, and for Ellie, who was doing her best at my home with the baby.

Mazz called to see how I was. "I can't believe it," she said. "I have another friend who has also been diagnosed with the same as you. I ought to put you in touch."

"Oh no, that's awful, Mazz."

"I know. She's on tour with *Hairspray* at the mo. She's the actress who took over as Killer Queen when I left *We Will Rock You*. She's been fitting her chemo round her *Hairspray* tour dates."

"Mazz, are you kidding? You mean Brenda Edwards? She was on *Loose Women* last week on the day of my first chemo and it was because I was watching her talking about positive mental attitude that I made the decision that if she can do it, then I can too."

Mazz put us in touch, and Brenda and I began chatting on Facebook Messenger. She seemed as pleased as me to be connecting with someone going through it as well. We shared our experiences. She was also enduring the cold cap and gave me tips. I talked her through her scheduled mastectomy. Apparently, mastectomy can take place either before or after chemotherapy. She described how she sang in the car as she drove to her chemo treatments and got her nurses singing too. We joked around a bit and compared photos of what chemo had done to our fingernails. Her upbeat attitude was a huge boost to me, and I was very pleased to connect with her.

Dominic took everything in his stride and continued his daily routine as usual, seeming almost unaware that I wasn't feeling great.

In between these hospital days, I tried to follow a normal routine and did the school runs, chatting with mums in the playground, where they always asked for an update and offered help. I tried to ignore the strange metallic taste in my mouth and the permanent queasiness.

Some days I felt so well that I invited Dom's friends and their mums round after school. The children messed about in the garden while we drank tea and chatted.

I was touched to receive a wooden engraved box from Surangi. Following her instructions, I wrote down two wishes, drew my reiki symbols, and placed them in the box together. Although she is a GP, she is also a believer in the magic of reiki. Obviously, I wished for a swift return to health, and felt blessed to have such a steadfast friendship. Surangi continued to offer a calm and pragmatic listening ear as well as managing school pick-ups and bringing me soup.

I experienced a range of side effects, such as numbness in the fingers, nausea, brittle dull hair, discoloured nails, and weight gain. However, although there were days when the toxins had built up in my system, making me feel bad, in the main I was ploughing through treatment and began ticking off the weeks. I got to know many of the regulars on the oncology ward. They were there for various cancers at different stages, many in a far worse state than me, and I reminded myself that I was one very lucky lady.

Spiritual Help and Healing
May 2016

Outside Marlow and just beyond the picturesque village of Frieth stood an old convent. It was the perfect place for the session of reiki healing. I had been recommended to see a healer, Sarah, and told she was the real deal. She welcomed me into an oak panelled room with high ceilings. Sarah seemed down to earth and genuine. Explaining that she only treats cancer patients, she switched her phone to some recorded music and asked me to climb onto a treatment table in the middle of the room. She held her hands above me and then, starting with my head, gradually worked her way down my body as I shut my eyes and tried to concentrate. I could feel her hands causing a strange buzzing sensation and a lot of pressure and I thought she must be pressing very hard on my stomach. I peeked, and her hand was some eighteen inches above my body. She wasn't even touching me.

After the treatment she reported she had felt a huge knot in my stomach area, a lot of tension and anxiety, and that it was blocked. Mentioning the pushing feeling I had experienced, she said she had unblocked the chakra and that it should now shift and be much more comfortable. My stomach, which felt like a tight ball of worry and made me nauseous ever since I had found the lump, suddenly relaxed. Maybe I was imagining it, but I was certainly feeling calmer. My own reiki training had taught me this healing really worked, but I was not expecting such a strong physical reaction.

Sarah explained, "I feel you are here not because you have cancer – because your cancer has gone – but because we are clearing all the negative energy of the past and travelling now to a positive place where you can plan and move forward. All the clearing you have been doing is for a purpose. To get rid of the bad stuff in your life. This IS the end of that period. When I see breast cancer sufferers, most times they have been in unhappy marriages or bad relationships. It is nice working with you as one who is not terminal and will be okay."

I spoke to her about Robin. "My brother has a terminal brain tumour. He has already defied the odds as he was told two years ago that he would not survive that long."

Sarah offered to see Robin.

Robin and I were also sharing and comparing notes. He was having a far tougher time than me and we were all very worried about him. He had just undergone a risky operation to reduce the size of his tumour but was feeling well enough to come with me to meet Sarah the reiki healer.

I drove him to the old convent. Whilst he was being treated, I went for a walk round the building. The convent was such a silent place with quite a strange atmosphere. I found an old library and ventured in. Cup of tea in hand, I began browsing through the old books on the shelves. I was about to take a book out to look at when I sensed a strange presence behind me and felt so prickly and uncomfortable that I left the room fast.

I found out later from a psychic medium friend that the room was haunted. "That's just the Colonel," she informed me. "He sometimes gets stroppy when people go into his library. He's okay, just has times he isn't happy to be disturbed. Just say 'Morning, Colonel' and you will be fine!"

On the way home Robin and I had our first of many discussions about life after death. I shared my absolute belief in the continuation of life after physical death. I was trying to explain to him about my messages from Rosie and tears ran down his cheeks. From that day onwards we became very close, and his spiritual awakening began. He was quite emotional when he left his session with Sarah. She is not only a healer but also has an incredible psychic ability and that day she brought Robin's childhood friend through. He had died a few years before and came back to see Robin. She even channelled his name. Rosie made her presence felt too and Robin now believed it really was true, that death was nothing to fear, although he told me many times he was still terrified of the dying process.

Each time we visited Sarah, the messages she delivered from the spirit world calmed his fears and our trips became a source of great comfort to us both. We would stop at a little café on the way home and share cake and cups of tea and discuss everything.

I wished I could do more for him, but ultimately these special times we shared helped to give him inner strength to face the inevitable.

Halfway
June 2016

It was now June, and Dr Thanvi congratulated me on my progress so far. I was concerned that I had gained a stone in weight being pumped with steroids every week. "Don't worry," he said. "I am confident you will shed that when it is over. You see, you do NOT have cancer anymore. This chemotherapy is now precautionary. You are at the halfway mark and having completed nine weekly sessions with nine to go, your last chemo will be August 22nd. You will have a month's break and then five weeks of radiotherapy every day. You can book a good holiday at the end of August." I couldn't thank him enough.

Carrie and I met for a coffee in the hospital canteen. She and I were such good friends now. Many ladies on our ward had formed close friendships and we had a giggle at some of the names they had given themselves such as *The Chemo Kittens* and *Breast Friends*. I was so glad that I had met so many of them, although I wish it had been under better circumstances.

By July the side effects seemed to be building up. My hands were continuously burning and wouldn't work properly. I struggled to open a can of beans and had burning eyes, numb, sore toes, and a red rash. Dr Thanvi ordered a two-week break from chemo to allow things to settle.

Carrie knocked on my front door. "Hey, Carrie, how are you doing?"

"I have to show you this. Are you ready?" she said as I shut the front door.

She whipped off her short blonde wig. "Here I am, Carrie, cancer patient!"

Carrie was completely bald. I said she looked okay, but she did not feel okay, and the previous day had asked her daughter to take the clippers to her almost bald head and finish the job properly. I felt guilty that I still had most of mine and imagined how awful it must have been to watch it fall. What started as a quick cup of tea and commiserations over the loss of her blonde locks extended to almost a whole day together with a lovely lunch overlooking the river, sharing our cancer experience but a lot more too.

I sneaked in another session with Sarah the healer. She was doing me so much good. As well as a healing session, she also gave me an impromptu reading. Rosie came through and she told me things Rosie was saying which she could not have known.

"Rose quartz crystal is great for healing," she said.

"Where can I get some of that, Sarah?"

"Don't go out and buy any. Some will find its way to you soon, I think."

The Gift
August 2016

By August I felt well enough to join my group of school mum friends, so we packed up fifteen kids and a lot of food and rented three yurts for another glamping weekend on the South Downs. The children spent hours playing cricket, running wild, watching the cows being milked, paddling in the sea at West Wittering Beach, and creating sand channels for the sea to wash away. As they played, we barbecued sausages, put the world to rights, discussed education, defused kids' squabbles, and drank prosecco. They were a few blissful days of warm sunshine and fresh country air, and I revelled in being with my friends, trying not to think that next week I would be back in the oncology ward again.

The first day back in chemo was as hard as I had expected. My eyebrows and lashes had fallen out. In fact, I looked a complete mess, and Jane the breast care nurse ushered me into a quiet room where I had a massive meltdown. She was sympathetic and suggested I arrange some counselling.

Back into my cold cap and hooked up to my chemo drip stand for my fifteenth treatment, I began to chat to a lovely lady called Carmen. She was an old timer on the ward, but our paths had never crossed. We immediately found common ground.

She said, "I'm big on what I call fairies."

I said, "I'm big on what I call spirit."

It was truly a match made in heaven! We chatted about angels, healing, crystals, past life regression, and so much more in the space of about forty-five minutes and I felt I had known her from somewhere before, so it was quite strange. Her zest for life was magnetic and I was full of admiration as she had been fighting her illness for several years and yet was so full of optimism. We exchanged mobile numbers.

The next week Carmen arrived in oncology carrying a heavy gift bag.

"This is a gift for you," she said.

The nurse who was inserting my cannula said, "Is she your friend?"

"She is now." I laughed.

The bag was so heavy, and since I was attached to a drip, she helped me to open it, revealing a huge piece of pink rose quartz with a candle in the middle. The healing crystal had found its way to me just as Sarah had predicted.

Following Dr Thanvi's earlier suggestion, I booked a holiday to Portugal with Ellie, Matt, Tabitha, and Dominic. It was exactly what I needed to get my weakened body back into shape – rest, relaxation, and sun.

The hotel was lovely, and Dom wanted to go for a swim as soon as we arrived. I put on my post mastectomy swimsuit and slid in a prosthetic gel fake boob. The pool side was full of young mums with great figures, and I suddenly felt self-conscious and overweight. I wore a shirt over my costume for the rest of the stay. I wasn't expecting to feel so sensitive and tired throughout the week's holiday. Maybe it was the build-up of the chemo. While it had done its job in wiping out the cancer, it had also wiped me out. I tried to act normally but felt okay one minute and exhausted the next. I owed it to my seven-year-old boy not to spoil his holiday and decided to resist the urge to write a massive *F*** CANCER* in the sand in case he saw. It was not fair that he had to put up with my illness over the past six months.

Goodbye Chemo
September 2016

September heralded the end of the chemo. I was ecstatic although oddly panicked that the weekly trips to the oncology ward were over. I developed a good relationship with several of the nurses and goodbye was bittersweet. I was indebted to them and had learned so much about human goodness. Over the past eighteen weeks, one of the patients who I had come to know and like had sadly passed away. Not everyone was as lucky as me.

I underwent thirty-five daily radiotherapy sessions, which compared to chemotherapy was a walk in the park. They just made me tired and gave me angry burn marks, but eventually they subsided, and the sessions were over. Dr Thanvi prescribed ongoing medication.

After eighteen months living with us, Ellie, Matt, and Tabitha moved out. It was time for them to be a normal family unit again and they settled into a new home nearby. Following reconstructive surgery in 2017, I gradually eased myself back into the normal world. I owed everything to Ms Shrotria, Dr Thanvi, and the nurses who continued to treat long-term cancer patients and those arriving to take up membership of a club nobody wanted to be a part of.

Royal Albert Hall
April 2017

Rosie's Rainbow Fund was very fortunate to be the recipient of a generous grant from Global's Make Some Noise. This led to some exciting opportunities to promote Rosie's work on radio and across other media. One morning I had a call from Global's Make Some Noise. I had been selected to represent Rosie's Rainbow Fund at an important concert given by Classic FM at the Royal Albert Hall. This was to be broadcast live on Classic FM radio. Hosted by John Suchet and Margherita Taylor, I was to speak about Rosie and the work we carry out in her name and how the money raised by Global's Make Some Noise had helped small charities like ours to really make a difference.

Arriving at the Royal Albert Hall accompanied by Bev, my friend and long-serving trustee of the charity, it was clear that this was an important benchmark in the history of Rosie's charity.

Bev Crook and Carolyn

Ushered to the stage for a sound check and to meet John and Margherita, I watched from the wings as the Classic FM orchestra were rehearsing. I looked out at the vast, empty 5,000-seat theatre and in my head asked Rosie to please get me through this without getting tongue-tied. It was a big deal, and they were expecting a full house.

In a dressing room, being kept calm by Bev, I changed into a long midnight blue sequinned dress and then it was time. Margherita and John stood with us in the wings. "You will be fine," they said.

In all the years of talking about Rosie at public events, this was a defining moment. As I stepped out onto the huge stage and was introduced by John Suchet there was applause from the full house. I spoke with pride about Rosie and how her legacy continues to make music for sick children, just as she wanted. Rosie and I received an applause from 5,000 concert-goers, and I have never been so proud.

Robin's Rainbow
May 14th, 2018

As I regained my strength, Robin's health was failing. He gradually and agonisingly lost the ability to speak and express himself. My mother was in denial but remained stoic, always coming up with ideas of how to help his failing communication. When I visited him, we would enjoy watching *Long Island Medium* on TV together. It brought him solace, I think.

Robin lost his five-year battle with brain cancer in 2018. On the morning of his death, his youngest daughter, Molly-May, texted me a photo of a rainbow which had just appeared at her feet. She was at university, revising for her final law exams. Robin passed into spirit two hours later.

It was May 14th, the same date Rosie had passed. It was yet another rainbow at a poignant moment and we believe it was no coincidence that Robin chose the same date and that Rosie had come to collect him.

Epilogue
June 2022

Nineteen years have passed since Rosie left us and thirteen years since that momentous day when our miracle baby son arrived. There are days when I look back at what we all endured and wonder how we ever got through such a terrible ordeal.

Mum celebrated her ninety-second birthday. The whole family reunited for a garden party. Because of the pandemic it was the first time we had all been together for two and a half years. In that time two new babies had joined our family.

My nieces, Alice and Harriet, had produced Ivy, now two, and Alfie, fourteen months, and we met for the first time, making this an extra special day for us all.

Bunting hung from the trees and the garden was alive with laughter and small children, the next generation who Rosie would never have the joy of knowing.

My sister-in-law Fiona and I were in Mum's kitchen. Fiona was whisking double cream. Feeling both happy and empty at the same time, I was silent as I watched her.

She stopped whisking and said, "I feel it too. It's so strange that this is such a happy day, but it feels wrong because our little Rosie should be here too."

She was suddenly teary. I had tears in my eyes too because she echoed exactly what I was feeling.

Fiona said, "You know it's like we have the most wonderful cake, but there is an ingredient missing. Those who never tasted the cake before with that added ingredient would never know there was something missing. But for those of us who had tasted the same cake with the added ingredient, we will know it will never taste quite right."

Her arms were round me, with both of us in that moment feeling the ache.

Then little Alfie, her grandson, my great nephew, toddled into the kitchen, his curly golden hair bobbing.

"But life goes on." I sighed. She smiled and nodded, and we both joined the rest of the family in Mum's garden…

Writing this book brought up a lot of memories which had remained buried because it was simply too painful. I am not entirely sure how I endured so much loss, but I did, and I am okay, and my surviving children are fine.

I am grateful that I am now healthy and can enjoy my two grandchildren. My little granddaughter Tabitha Rose is now six. A grandson, Maximilian Robin, arrived in 2019, named after my beloved brother Robin.

Rosie's cousins grew up. They have been through university, forged careers, some have found partners, and some have had children. I will always wonder what Rosie would be doing now. Would she be a wonderful mummy, or maybe be enjoying an interesting career? There will always be unanswered questions and years of family gatherings she will never get to share.

When my granddaughter Tabitha was three, she had been swimming in the pool in Mum's garden. Ellie reported that when she had asked who had been in the pool with her, Tabitha said, "Oh, only me and Rosie."

It is commonly reported that small children can see spirit, so who knows, perhaps Rosie was there that day. I wish Rosie could have known her big sister's children, but maybe she does. I am certain she is still very much around.

Since the death of my daughter, I can truthfully say there is never a day when I do not think of her, long for her, and miss her more than I can say. I accept that will never change and neither would I wish it to. I live with it, and I still have days when the agony returns, and it feels as though I am right back at the beginning. Yes, it hurts. But I have learnt through many years of practice and survival that tomorrow can feel lighter and I can pull myself from that dark place which used to swallow me up. I can be happy in a different way while that hard stone of grief remains embedded and permanent. Now it exists in a place where most of the time it just lives within me. Unimaginable loss has changed me, and all our family. I often wonder what we would have been like had life not dealt us such hard blows. But it has made us who we are now.

Rosie's Rainbow Fund continues to prosper. The charity has raised well over £2 million through fundraising and generous donations from schools, businesses, and kind individuals. We are always grateful for every penny we receive and as a small charity we can ensure that all our donations go straight to the children and families Rosie wished to help. Our resources are always stretched to the limit, but we continue to carry on making magic, music, and rainbows.

Bev, Helene, and Candice remained dedicated trustees of Rosie's charity for nineteen years. Our friendship is stronger than ever. Helene's grief for Ella is like mine for Rosie, quieter now but always there. Our charity work helps so many, and it hurts me that there will always be ill children, but Rosie's Rainbow shines very brightly and remains a lifesaver for many children and parents. I am proud of all we have achieved in the name of my beautiful, funny, headstrong, talented, and beloved younger daughter.

Hundreds of children have trained at Redroofs since Rosie left us. Eventually there were children coming through our school who had never met Rosie. Redroofs is still thriving and always full of music song and creative ventures. The celebration of childhood remains the ethos of our school. Happy, healthy children are the most important thing. Memories made in our school are precious and childhood too fleeting to waste.

Dominic and I moved house last year. I was brave enough to offload large boxes of Rosie's clothes which I kept in the loft boxed up and labelled. Her Redroofs uniform, pyjamas, even underwear had remained frozen in time for eighteen years and it was the moment to bid them goodbye. I couldn't bear to think of anyone wearing them, so the boxes were discarded unopened, and that felt okay. My girl's precious Beanies were given to Ellie for Tabitha to play with. Rosie won't be needing them or maybe she will be there in spirit as her niece enjoys them.

I recently found the book given to me by the local Rabbi all those years ago, *When Bad Things Happen to Good People*. I now understand that they really do. I decided to pass the book on because it is time and someone else may need it now.

Whilst clearing the loft for the house move, I stumbled upon a notebook under a pile of yellowing papers. It was from 1995 and the holiday in Cornwall and contained the psychic prediction of the birth of another child after a long gap. Proof once again that this was always going to be. The sacrifice was huge, but somehow we survived.

Dominic is a teenager now and older than Rosie when she left us. He is much taller than me and thriving at senior school. He is bright and popular with lots of friends. He is something of an animal whisperer, which is fascinating when we know that his egg donor was a veterinary surgeon in Moldova. I have made it my job to drip feed information to Dom about his story and how he came about and how very special he is. He has grown up knowing his backstory and he takes it all in his stride. Occasionally he asks for more information, which I readily share, and he enjoys hearing about it but only in small doses before he turns his attention back to his Xbox, his latest chat with his mates, or asking, "What's for tea, Mum? Can we order a pizza?"

Somewhere out there is a woman living a very different life in Moldova who made this all possible and who is probably completely unaware that a baby boy was born from her egg donation, and she will not know that her generosity on that day in April 2008 changed our lives. Maybe one day my son will want to trace this lady or maybe not. Dominic can choose. He asks about Rosie sometimes, but like most thirteen-year-old boys he lives firmly in the now and that is exactly how it should be.

I carry on with Rosie beside and within me in everything I do. She has stage managed me through every twist and turn of this impossible, joyful, strange, difficult, exciting, challenging production which we call life. She sits on her director's chair high on her rainbow, and she never ever lets me down. I am healthy, we are all fine, and life goes on.

I look forward now with optimism and await the next chapter, hoping it will be happy, healthy, and productive. Despite all that has happened, I firmly believe that *The Future is Rosie*.

Top Left: Sister Sam and Mum June.

Top Right: Carolyn and June.

Centre: Carolyn,Ludovic, Sam and Robin.

Left: Dominic today.

Acknowledgements

Starting as a random collection of jottings poured out as a sort of cathartic diary, the beginnings of my memoir were saved (luckily) onto my computer and in umpteen notebooks and scraps of paper since 2003. Eventually I decided to turn them into my story.

My dear friend Allison Cairns offered to type up the box files full of 180,000 words of rantings and ramblings. Thank you, Allison, not only for the weeks of wading through thousands of pages in between having Dom for sleepovers with your boys, but also for your knowledge that we all have the power within us to make things happen. We have both learned it is no coincidence that people come into our lives for a reason!

Last year my sister Sam bought me an online memoir writing course for my birthday. This was the kick start I needed to begin shaping my book. I am grateful to Cathy Rentzenbrink for sharing such expertise and to Shannon Leone Fowler for your useful feedback and mentoring.

My search for a publisher began in February 2022 when I submitted my memoir to a host of publishing companies. When I fortuitously found Janet Weitz, who runs Alliance Publishing Press, it turned out we had already met, that she already knew about me and Rosie, and had even attended our Rosie's Rainbow Fund charity shows. There was an instant connection, and I signed a contract with Alliance Publishing Press.

Commencing the edit, I assumed naively we would just correct a few typos and agree a cover design. It was as far from the truth as I could imagine.

Janet said, "I'd like to think we've birthed this book together" and this is what we did. You have been an extraordinary mentor in this labour of love. I have revelled in every second of our intense working days together. Thank you will never be enough for all I have learned from you and for enabling this book to happen. Barry Weitz, your help has been hugely appreciated as have our discussions and your feedback over your beautifully catered lunches.

Thanks to all the team at Alliance Publishing Press who have invested a wealth of expertise into my book. I am so fortunate to have been able to access your outstanding talents and skills.

To all the friends featured in my book, you have played your own huge roles in helping me write my memoir. A special thanks to Valerie Weyland. Without your encouragement there may not have even been an IVF story.

Heartfelt thanks to the special people in my book, Gaenor Clarke, Beverly Crook, Helene Czornyj, Candice Eales, Phil Eastabrook, Dee Hounsom, Shirley Jones, Jodie Lewis, Gaynor Mullings, Mazz Murray, Gina Murray, Jayne O Mahoney, Ceridwen Rees, Machiel Roets, Adam Stafford, Surangi Suriarachchi, Jenni Thomas OBE, Amanda Tibbels, and to Carrie Cotter and Carmen Lester, my 'cancer buddies'.

To Lucy Benjamin and Joanne Froggatt, my appreciation for all you continue to do so generously and with such selflessness. I am so proud of you two amazing women.

Relaying my journey over the course of time, many friends have said, "Honestly you couldn't write it – but you should!" With countless coffees, dog walks, cuppas in, and meals out as I kept you up to date with my progress, you have always been there ready to listen and give me confidence. You are all part of my story. Thank you.

To David, although we are no longer together, we have shared all three of our children, the joy as well as the grief. Your cooperation with elements of this memoir is much appreciated.

For my late brother Robin – in admiration and love – you taught me so much about courage and true goodness.

Sam, you have been an endless inspiration and a push to my shove. You are always there not just as a sister but as a sounding board, ideas factory, and driving force.

My love and thanks to all my family, to my mum June, and also my daughter Ellie for being so supportive through the writing process and in allowing me to tell our story.

To my son Dominic, thanks for putting up with your mum over the past months writing and editing into the early hours.

And finally thank you, Rosie. You continue to be my inspiration. Your motto in life was 'Don't talk about it. DO IT' and I hope you are proud that your mummy finally did.

CPSIA information can be obtained
at www.ICGtesting.com
Printed in the USA
BVHW050316310123
657511BV00017B/89

9 781838 259839